MISSED VOLUME 1 AND 2 OF OUR TRACK ck
Visit *www.brmm.ag/*
Visit *www.brmm.ag/*

Medium Layouts

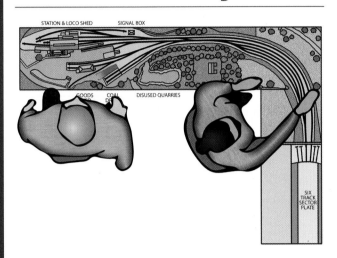

76 TALYLLYN ROAD

66 COTTLESTON
68 BACKDORE QUAY
70 THISTLEMERE
72 SALMON PASTURES
74 ALSTON
78 TAPLEY

80 LOFTUS ROAD
82 BEECHES TMD
86 ABERDARE
88 GOLDHANGER
90 DALESIDE PARKWAY
92 CHEDDAR
94 CULM

Large Layouts

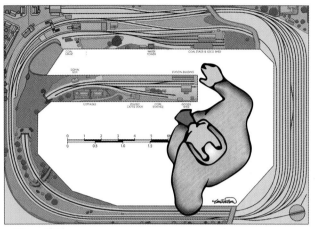

98 LONGDREM

102 TETLEYS MILLS
104 TRENTHAM JUNCTION
106 ELGIN

100 ASTON

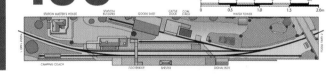

96 PENMAENMAWR

108 KINETON

WELCOME

Oil Drum Lane (OO) p13

BRITISH RAILWAY MODELLING

BRITISH RAILWAY MODELLING
is published by Warners Group Publications plc
T 01778 392059 **E** BRM@warnersgroup.co.uk

SUBSCRIPTION ENQUIRIES
T 01778 392002

DIGITAL EDITION ENQUIRIES
E help@pocketmags.com

EDITORIAL
I MANAGING EDITOR Andy McVittie
E andy.mcvittie@warnersgroup.co.uk
I EDITOR Howard Smith
E howards@warnersgroup.co.uk
I FEATURES WRITER Phil Parker
E phil@pagenumberone.co.uk
I RMWEB EDITOR & BRM PHOTOGRAPHER
Andy York **I** **E** info@rmweb.co.uk
I TRACKPLAN ILLUSTRATOR
Ian Wilson at Pacific Studio
E ian@pacificstudio.co.uk

I PUBLISHER Steve Cole
E stevec@warnersgroup.co.uk
I MARKETING MANAGER Carly Dadge
E carlyd@warnersgroup.co.uk

ADVERTISING
I GROUP ADVERTISING MANAGER Bev Machin
T 01778 392055
E bevm@warnersgroup.co.uk
I SALES EXECUTIVE Allison Mould
T 01778 395002
E allison.mould@warnersgroup.co.uk

DESIGN AND PRODUCTION
I DESIGNERS
James Teather
E jamest@warnersgroup.co.uk
Ruth Jamieson
E ruth.jamieson@warnersgroup.co.uk
I ADVERTISING DESIGNER & PRODUCTION
Viv Lane **T** 01778 392453
E viv.lane@warnersgroup.co.uk

DISTRIBUTION
TRADE ACCOUNT SALES
Natalie Cole **T** 01778 392404
E tradeaccountorders@warnersgroup.co.uk
I UK/OVERSEAS NEWSTRADE SALES
Keiron Jefferies **T** 01778 395043
E keironj@warnersgroup.co.uk
I NEWSTRADE DISTRIBUTION
Tom Brown 01778 391135
ISSN 0968-0764

I PRINTING
Warners (Midlands) plc, The Maltings,
West Street, Bourne, Lincolnshire PE10 9PH

H ello readers and a very warm welcome to this third volume of the **BRM** Guide to Trackplans and Layout Design. Read on to help ensure your next layout is an entertaining one, full of well-designed features and built on solid foundations.

It's exciting to think that **BRM** will celebrate its 25th anniversary next year, but with that comes an advantage; I've been able to delve into our archives and discover great trackplans from layouts we've featured over the years to share with you - some large, some small, some elaborate, others surprisingly simple.

The owners of the designs featured inside have told us from practical experience what works and what doesn't, so you avoid their mistakes. You'll find this useful information alongside our helpful 'Pros' and 'Cons' panel that'll make you pause for thought and reflect on how you can take elements from each to improve your design.

In our two previous volumes, I've covered the variety of scales and gauges available and we've shared advice on optimising space around your house to fit your layout, along a host of other useful tips. If you missed these two previous volumes, I'd recommend downloading them as digital editions today. Visit *www.pocketmags. com/BRM* to collect your copies.

Despite a scale included with every trackplan inside, it's not always evident to visualise their size, so we've dropped some scale people alongside to give you a better idea.

Avoiding previously trodden ground, you'll find this volume has more space for additional trackplans alongside useful advice from planning experts Paul Lunn and Ian Wilson. So, turn over, let's get your project started.

Editor | Howard Smith

Ideas for contributions should be sent in outline form to the Editor for consideration. Please clearly mark all material with your name and address, and include sufficient postage if you require material to be returned. Views expressed by contributors are not necessarily those of the Editor or Publisher. From time to time Warners lend reputable companies the names and addresses of readers who have responded to offers, services and competitions organised by BRM. If you do not wishto receive such mailings, please write to Warners Group Distribution, Dept WD, Manor Lane, Bourne, Lincolnshire PE10 9PH or call 01778 391153.

Cheddar (P4) p92

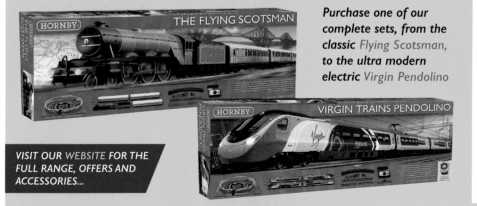

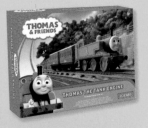

OIL DRUM LANE

With a collection of DRS-liveried locomotives to display, Mark Murray drew inspiration from exhibition layouts for his present-day diesel depot.

On a sunny day, Mark visited his local Freightliner depot at Midland Road in Leeds to take photographs. He witnessed two Class 66s in DRS livery and thought about building a depot layout.

DRS has two depots, one at Kingmoor in Carlisle and one in Crewe where maintenance is carried out. 'Oil Drum Lane' represents a fictitious depot located somewhere between the two, but making use of commonly seen features around depots.

Mark used Peco code 100 track with points operated by Seep motors. The layout is DCC operated, advisable with a depot layout to reduce the number of isolation switches required with DC layouts.

Buildings and structures are scratch-built, but the engine sheds and fuel tanks are from Bachmann Scenecraft. Creating the sheds required cutting a single Bachmann Scenecraft shed in two. Consider this technique if space is tight on your layout - you don't always need to represent buildings in their entirety. ∎

Pros
- Three-way point requires less space
- A kickback fuelling point fills an empty area

Cons
- Layout is purely a way of displaying locomotives with limited movement - consider a passing mainline for more interest

Factfile

Layout name: Oil Drum Lane
Scale/gauge: OO gauge
Size: 9ft x 1ft 10in
Era/region: Present
Location: Ficticious Depot in West Midlands
Layout type: Fiddleyard to MPD
Owner: Mark Murray
Photography: Andy York

Trackplan

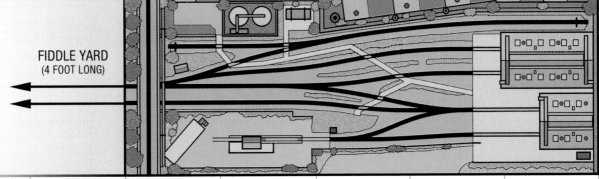

OIL TANKS   LOW RELIEF FACTORY BUILDINGS

FIDDLE YARD
(4 FOOT LONG)

DIESEL FUEL &
INSPECTION PIT

MAINTENANCE
SHEDS

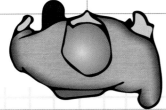

OO GAUGE

PETER'S STREET

Pete Harvey's compact OO gauge exhibition layout depicts a modern terminus station set in the West Midlands.

A decade ago after the Warley Show, Pete Harvey wondered what challenge to set himself for the coming year. He settled on building a new layout, working on a fictional trackplan, but set in the West Midlands around the Cannock area. Overall, it's size was 8ft x 1ft.

Early on during its build, Pete wanted to be able to move trains around in the fiddleyard and to be able to do this he would need a double slip. This also meant he'd need sidings in both directions, so he included these into the scenic area of the layout. As such, items of rolling stock could change during a day's running, all hidden underneath the road bridge.

The two tracks entering the station form a crossover. One has a small siding headshunt with a platform. The shorter of the two platforms accommodates a two-car unit, whilst the longer can take a three-car unit. Trains depart on the opposite line to that on which they enter. ■

Pros

I Compact layout that's quick to build
I Track isn't parallel and overbridge isn't perpendicular with layout boards which helps break up their linear appearance

Cons

I Limited operational possibilities with mulltiple units operating on a 'one in - one out' policy, but occasionally a locomotive can be parked at the rear

Factfile

Layout name: Peter's Street
Scale/gauge: OO gauge
Size: 4ft x 1ft (plus fiddleyard)
Era/region: 2000s
Location: West Midlands
Layout type: Fiddleyard to terminus
Owner: Pete Harvey
Photography: Andy York
See more: September 2014 **BRM**

Trackplan

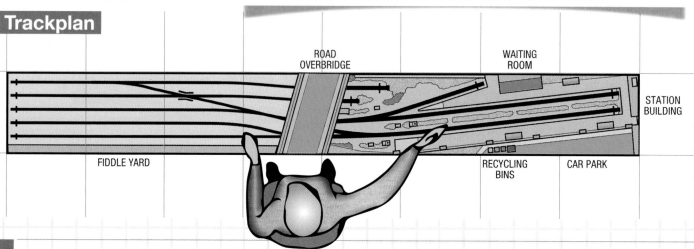

ROAD OVERBRIDGE

WAITING ROOM

STATION BUILDING

FIDDLE YARD

RECYCLING BINS

CAR PARK

HARTBURN

Foregoing the temptations of US HO, Ian Manderson built this EM gauge North British branch instead.

Hartburn didn't start as a remote Northumberland branch line. Its builder was planning a new US HO layout based on the Richmond, Fredericksburg and Potomac railroad, but upon returning after an exhibition, thoughts of a small US test track were replaced with planning something based in rural Northumberland in EM gauge. His two baseboards became three and Ian realised how much bigger 4mm : 1ft scale is compared to 3.5mm : 1ft scale.

He retained his original idea of running the layout at home to relax, but his thoughts turned to portability, lighting setups, backscenes and things closely associated with an exhibition layout. He also wanted to experiment with scenery.

More used to modelling urban 'grime', the thought of modelling rural embankments and hedges filled him with dread and to make things a little harder, Ian felt the need to portray the layout set in late autumn without bright green fields, opting for muted tones instead.

The layout's three baseboards each measure 4ft x 1ft, but fiddle yards at each end are different - one end houses a sector plate, the other a traverser. The traverser is made from drawer mechanisms from a DIY outlet, but Ian admits that a wider baseboard would have made finding runners easier. ∎

Factfile

Layout name: Hartburn
Scale/gauge: 4mm:1ft / EM gauge
Size: 12ft x 1ft (including fiddleyards)
Era/region: early 1960s, British Railways
Location: rural Northumberland
Layout type: Fiddleyard to fiddleyard
Owner: Ian Manderson
Photography: Ian Manderson
See more: October 2011 **BRM**

Pros

I No train timetable makes operations more frequent than reality
I Help from friends made the layout more enjoyable and easier to build
I Good project to develop new scenic skills

Cons

I Difficult to keep things moving to entertain the public with limited space

Trackplan

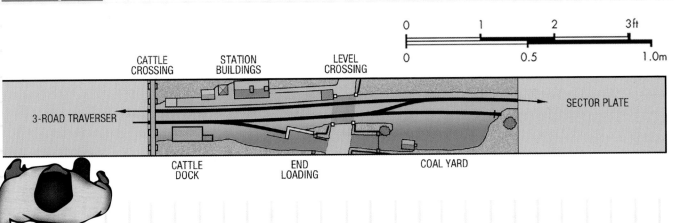

CATTLE CROSSING   STATION BUILDINGS   LEVEL CROSSING

0   1   2   3ft
0   0.5   1.0m

3-ROAD TRAVERSER

SECTOR PLATE

CATTLE DOCK   END LOADING   COAL YARD

HELLINGLY HOSPITAL

Phil Parker's compact layout provides a fascinating insight into the unusual operations of an internal railway at a hospital complex.

"Why build a model of an obscure line two hundred miles from where you live?" Phil Parker blames Peter Harding who wrote an excellent history of the line from Hellingly station to the psychiatric hospital. On the front cover there's a drawing of the unusual steeple-cab locomotive which caught his eye.

When it came to building the model, it had to be small enough to fit in a normal-sized room. It also had to travel in a car, the car in question being a VW Beetle which limited the length of the main scenic board to 4ft. Phil didn't want baseboard joints under the overhead as he suspected they'd be a problem. Fast set-up and little to carry to a show were also considerations. The line ran through attractive landscaped grounds, so the model needed to show a part of this as well as the more built-up area in the hospital.

The engine shed and water tower had to be included to set the location. The layout is set in 1900 when the contractors are on-site completing works. Electrification is underway and odd wagons can be seen delivering loads that otherwise wouldn't be present.

A fascia is built into the main board and incorporates a strip light - it's heavy, but provides a good level of illumination. Seen here is the second version of the layout - 6in shorter and 6in wider, the first version not fit into the beetle. Track was replaced with Peco as his attempts using SMP proved unsuccessful. ■

Pros

I A fascia board with integrated strip light offers better viewing at shows
I If at first you don't succeed, don't be afraid to try again using the same buildings

Cons

I No photographs of the prototype buildings left construction to the imagination
I The overhead catenary makes cleaning difficult - an electronic track cleaner is needed

Factfile

Layout name: Hellingly Hospital Railway
Scale/gauge: 4mm:1ft / OO gauge
Size: 4ft x 18in plus fiddleyards
Era/region: 1900s
Location: 20 miles east of Brighton
Layout type: Fiddleyard to fiddleyard
Owner: Phil Parker
Photography: Tony Wright
See more: June 2004 **BRM**

Trackplan

HELLINGLY HOSPITAL

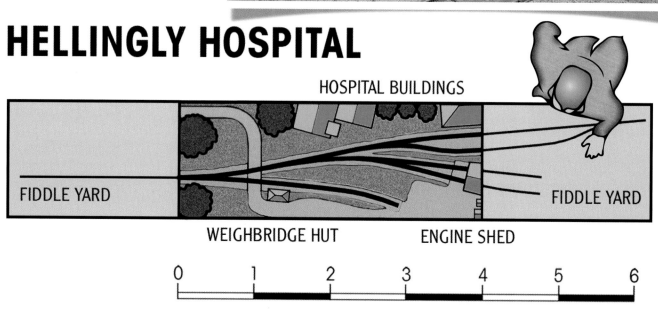

HOSPITAL BUILDINGS

FIDDLE YARD

WEIGHBRIDGE HUT

ENGINE SHED

FIDDLE YARD

0   1   2   3   4   5   6

ENIGMA ENGINEERING

Paul Gittins' shunting puzzle challenges its operator to order goods wagons around a minimum space layout.

Having modelled a compact north American layout, Paul Gittins felt he could copy the concept across to model the same layout with a British theme. To make things more interesting he built it in P4 gauge because he already had all the stock to hand.

The trackplan was drawn on a computer using Autocad. All track was handbuilt, points being made with a 24in radius, all of which could fit onto an A4 template sheet of paper. This makes the points quite tight, but the two-axle rolling stock and shorter locomotives cope with this fine.

Point operation is mechanical, the two central rear points each have a push rod made from a length of code 70 rail. It reduces costs, maintenance and failure rates.

The two sidings and the headshunt were intended to accept two wagons, but the runaround can accept four.

A card system is used when shunting the six wagons. Paul's design was to have the front of the layout lowered to form a canal basin, but ran out of time, so it was covered with grass.

During the early stages of planning when the track was being 'mocked up' on the baseboards, Paul realised that if he made the sidings only long enough for two wagons they'd look out of place. He overcame this by building them longer and shortening them artificially by placing a wagon turntable at the left-hand siding and gluing two rusty wagon wheels to the rails on the Enigma siding. The shunting challenge can be completed in 15 minutes with a good operator - 45 minutes if not so steady. ∎

Factfile

Layout name: Enigma Engineering
Scale/gauge: 4mm:1ft / P4 gauge
Size: 4ft x 1ft (plus fiddleyard)
Era/region: British Railways 1950s
Location: Ficticious, Black Country
Layout type: Fiddleyard to sidings
Owner: Paul Gittins
See more: November 2006 **BRM**

Pros ✓

I Overscale three-link couplings help operation without looking too out of place
I No controller required - power is pre-regulated and via a spring loaded switch

Cons ✗

I More effort required when planning length of sidings
I Handbuilt points were initially problematic - hand-built track requires extensive testing

Trackplan

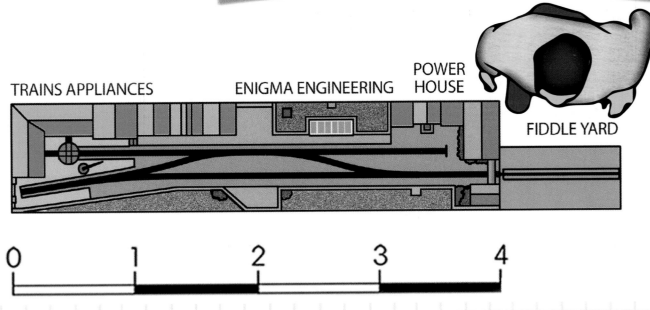

TRAINS APPLIANCES   ENIGMA ENGINEERING   POWER HOUSE   FIDDLE YARD

0   1   2   3   4

A W1400 dragline built by Ransomes & Rapier of Ipswich removing overburden – draglines had long jibs to move unwanted rock away from the ironstone workings. Note the side drilling taking place to loosen the limestone, drilling the ore bed ready for blasting to loosen the ore, and a power shovel preparing to load ore into railway wagons.

SEE A WORKING QUARRY

For a practical quarrying experience, visit the Rocks By Rail Museum near Cottesmore in Rutland. For more information see *www.rocks-by-rail.org*

IRONSTONE QUARRIES

Professional trackplan illustrator, Ian Wilson, explores the appeal of modelling ironstone railways, often located in pleasant rural countryside.

The earliest ironstone quarries were found where ore deposits lay close to the surface. Excavation was done manually by plank and barrow working, and loaded wagons of ore would be hauled by horse power. As quarrying became more intense, narrow-gauge steam-hauled systems sprang up and most – but not all – were replaced by standard gauge lines. Later quarrying used large draglines to remove overburden and reveal the iron ore seams for smaller excavators to load into railway wagons – then to be carried either directly to nearby steel works or to exchange sidings on the nearest main line railway.

Quarry Operation

The most intensive quarrying operations were around Corby in Northamptonshire, where the extensive quarry network was used to supply the blast furnaces of the massive Stewarts & Lloyds steelworks. My father worked in the Bessemer Plant there, so I was brought up in the shadow of the steelworks and within earshot of steam locomotives hard at work in a nearby quarry.

In Northamptonshire there were also smaller ironworks at Kettering, Cransley, Islip and Wellingborough. Here and at Corby the quarries were connected directly to the steelworks, mostly by standard gauge lines but at Kettering the gauge was 3ft 0in and at Wellingborough it was metre gauge. Ore from outlying quarries had to be loaded into main line wagons and marshalled at exchange sidings to be taken on to local or more distant ironworks.

In the quarries, tracks were lightly laid so they could be slewed sideways as excavation of the quarry progressed. One excavator – usually a dragline with sufficient jib length for tipping clear of a train awaiting loading – would remove the overburden and another, usually a shovel, would load the wagons at the quarry face. Lines often travelled through picturesque scenery before reaching the exchange sidings. Loaded trains from the quarry would amount to about eight wagons, often less and many quarries continued working into the mid-1970s so both industrial and main line diesels could be seen. Where rail access to quarries was impractical, lorries were used to bring ore to tipping docks at the exchange sidings.

For detailed information on all aspects of ironstone quarrying I recommend the series of nine books by Eric Tonks titled 'The Ironstone Quarries of the Midlands'.

The cover of an 8 page brochure promoting the 52-B Steam Quarry Shovel manufactured by Ruston-Bucyrus Ltd of Lincoln. One of these machines was presented to the Leicester Museum of Technology by W. H. McAlpine in 1972 and can be seen at the Museum's Abbey Pumping Station.

And so to some ideas for ironstone layouts – all based on prototype locations, but with a bit of license to make them work in model form. An essential requirement will be to have removable ore loads for all wagons!

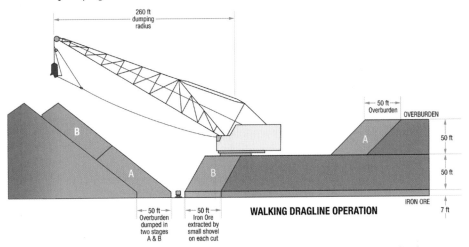

The extraction of iron ore by walking dragline. Note the amount of overburden compared with the quantity of ore.

Iron Ore – a geological history

Many years ago, the Earth's continents were closer together and changing shallow seas covered parts of Europe, including at times the east of England. Rivers carried sediment and dissolved minerals to the seas and lakes, where they were deposited. During this era, the Midlands were as far south as Biarritz or the French Riviera are now.

The outcrop of jurassic minerals - including Portland Stone, Oxford Clay, Northamptonshire Sand Ironstone, Lincolnshire Limestone, Frodingham Ironstone and Cleveland Ironstone - stretches from the Dorset coast to Middlesbrough in North East England. To the east of this is the outcrop of Cretaceous minerals - mainly chalk and limestone. The Northampton Sand Ironstone of the jurassic ridge is the principal ironstone bearing bed in the East Midlands, and the reason for the abundance of quarries in Northamptonshire, Leicestershire, Rutland and South Lincolnshire in the middle of the 20th century.

Sproxton

Sproxton was at the end of the eight mile long High Dyke branch, opened in 1916 to enable local ore to be supplied to steelworks further north, and is an example of the exchange sidings being very close to the quarry. It was owned by the Park Gate Iron &

Steel Co. and later by British Steel, Scunthorpe Division. Initially horses were used to haul loaded wagons to the exchange sidings, but as the quarry went deeper steam locomotives took over. They were stabled in an unusual creosoted timber military-style hut - surely a fire

risk, but it outlasted the quarry as the photos show. Usual power on the branch were Class O2 2-8-0s from Grantham Shed, and they often handed over their trains of loaded ore to 'Pacifics' at the main line exchange sidings.

The timber engine shed and office **(left)**, with the lorry garage **(top right)**. These photographs were taken in the early 1980s, about 10 years after closure. The trackbed leading to the exchange sidings is curved **(below)**, still evident in this view looking past the lorry garage with the weigh house on the left. The structures at Sproxton are all closely spaced together – perfect for modelling!

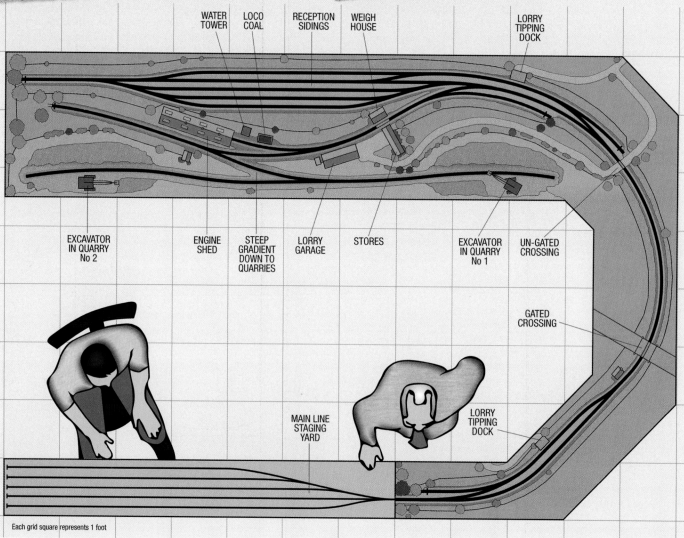

WATER TOWER · LOCO COAL · RECEPTION SIDINGS · WEIGH HOUSE · LORRY TIPPING DOCK

EXCAVATOR IN QUARRY No 2 · ENGINE SHED · STEEP GRADIENT DOWN TO QUARRIES · LORRY GARAGE · STORES · EXCAVATOR IN QUARRY No 1 · UN-GATED CROSSING

GATED CROSSING

MAIN LINE STAGING YARD

LORRY TIPPING DOCK

Each grid square represents 1 foot

Quarrying on the left hand (west) side of the main line ceased in 1950, and the bailey bridge seen under construction here was built to provide access to new quarries to the east. The narrow gauge lines were abandoned and replaced by lorries, which used the former engine shed as a garage.

Tilton station was on the Great Northern and London & North Western joint line from Market Harborough to Newark, a few miles south of Melton Mowbray. The isolated outcrop of ironstone was revealed by the building of the railway – which was in a deep cutting. The quarry railway system was 3ft gauge and ore was brought from the quarries in square steel tubs and tipped into waiting hopper wagons by a rotary tippler. Steam haulage was used between 1928 and 1950, at which time the supply of ore became exhausted and the quarry closed. A new quarry was then opened on the other side of the railway line but, road haulage replaced the narrow-gauge system and a bridge was built over the tracks to enable lorries to access the tipping dock. The main line wagons were rolled under the tipping dock by gravity, and then into sidings to await departure to Stanton Iron Works at Ilkeston.

Right: An overall view of the narrow gauge lines leading to the rotary tippler. Hopper wagons were run by gravity under the tippler to be loaded, then released to carry on by gravity into sidings in the station yard. The narrow gauge engine shed can be seen top left.

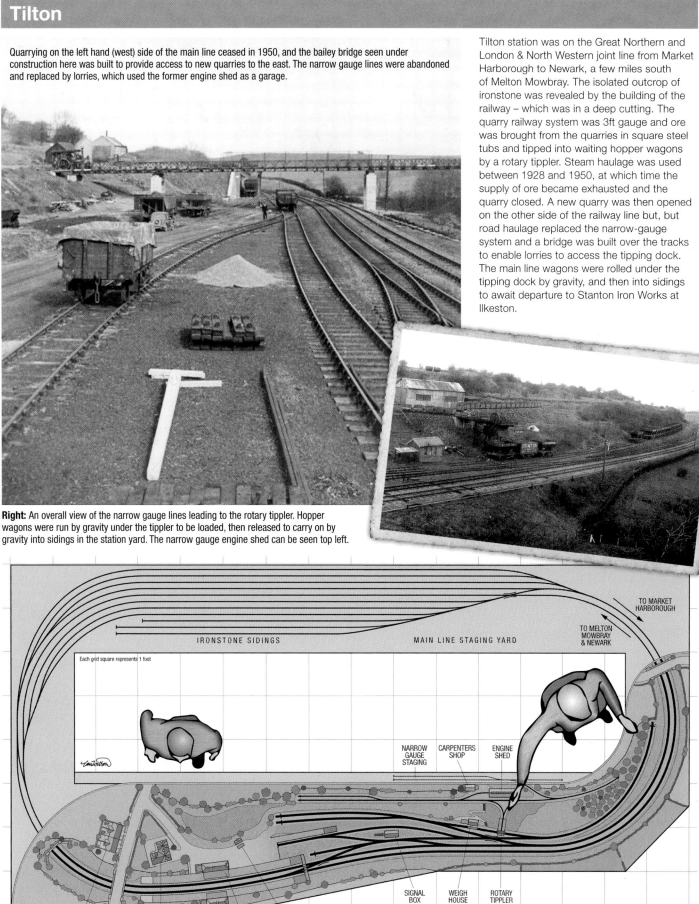

Storefield

Storefield was originally a 2ft 6in narrow gauge system which operated from 1902 until closure in 1929. In 1940 during World War II, the South Durham Steel & Iron Co. re-laid the system with standard gauge track and production of ore then continued until closure in 1971. In later years BR wagons were loaded at the quarry face and taken up the stiff climb to the exchange sidings alongside the Nottingham loop of the Midland between Kettering and Corby. Although the quarries were close to the steelworks at Corby, the ore was taken from Storefield to the South Durham steelworks at West Hartlepool, and in 1962, BR provided 500 vacuum-fitted 27 Ton iron ore tipplers for this service. Trains were mainly hauled by BR Class 9F 2-10-0s, but I can remember seeing 'Britannia' 4-6-2s in charge at times.

The accompanying sketch plan was drawn with a view to constructing a BRM project layout in 7mm scale, but had to be put on hold to make way for other projects. I tried to incorporate as many 'Storefield' features as possible but it would have been quite a squeeze in O gauge, and perhaps could be built in the same space but in a smaller scale.

Peckett 0-4-0ST 'Cockspur' takes 4 loaded tipplers up to the exchange sidings. Standard gauge Pecketts were not that common in the ironstone quarries. JOHN SCHOLES

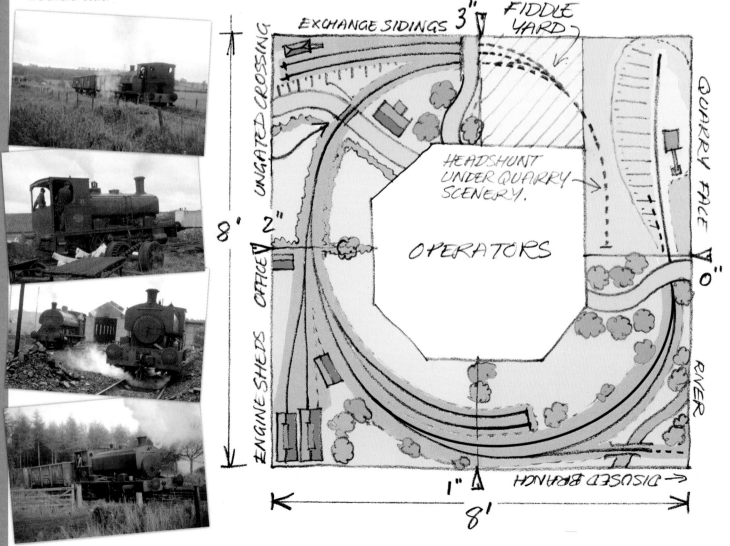

Bridgefield Quarries

Storefield is featured in an Ivo Peters video 'Ironstone Lines of the East Midlands' and this along with personal memories prompted me to build a 7mm scale model of an ironstone line, and to capture some of the character of the line. This is a small layout by O gauge standards, but has many of the features of Storefield – at one end a glimpse of the upper fiddle-yard exchange sidings and the rear of a Midland signal box suggests that they are alongside a main line. The line continues across an ungated crossing, dropping to a passing loop where full wagons from the quarries are exchanged for empties to be taken back for loading. The line passes under a road overbridge to reach the bottom fiddle-yard, which represents the quarries. The ruling gradient is 1-in-40, but the line to the engine shed falls away steeply at 1-in-18 – just as at Storefield. The model is still under construction – as the photographs show - but it's already booked to appear in future pages of **BRM**! ▨

A view looking towards the exchange sidings, with a Minerva Peckett 0-4-0ST in the loop with empties for the quarry. An Ixion Hudswell Clarke 0-6-0ST is seen at the water tank. A site for the quarry office is in the foreground.

Looking towards the engine shed and quarry road bridge. A Prototype Models Midland signal box is on the left and farm cottages by Allan Downes on the right. The site for quarry workers' cottages is on the left beyond the road.

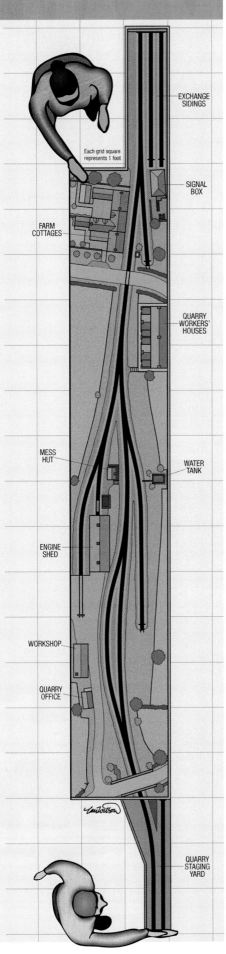

EXCHANGE SIDINGS

Each grid square represents 1 foot

SIGNAL BOX

FARM COTTAGES

QUARRY WORKERS' HOUSES

MESS HUT

WATER TANK

ENGINE SHED

WORKSHOP

QUARRY OFFICE

QUARRY STAGING YARD

KINGSWOOD

Armed with ideas, Wayne Webb set out to build an action-packed layout, but his plans changed as he started to lay track.

Back in 2005, at the age of 46, Wayne decided to take up railway modelling as a new hobby. The design for his first layout was based on Crawley Down (**BRM** June 2005) which he liked.

He established a list of what he wanted on the layout - an Up and Down mainline, a station, branchline, goods yard, coal yard and engine sheds. He drew a plan, but this changed when he started laying track and found he had more room on the boards than originally thought.

From the cattle dock, the siding joins with the single track goods line, which then doubles after the signal box. The track then passes under a road bridge out of sight, but would theoretically join the main line.

Wayne admits he's not entirely sure if the design of this part of the layout really works - his original plan was just a siding - but there's more space which helps with stock movements.

Fiddleyards are basic, with track continuing from the layout to an end stop, but are acceptable for home use. ∎

Pros

I Building this layout has given its builder the confidence to scratchbuild
I Lots of operational potential with sidings and a mainline

Cons

I Avoid overcrowding on small layouts
I Fiddleyards (not pictured) are basic and could be upgraded

Factfile

Layout name: Kingswood
Scale/gauge: N gauge
Size: 5ft x 2ft (plus fiddleyards)
Era/region: late 1930s
Location: Somewhere on GWR
Layout type: Fiddleyard to fiddleyard
Owner: Wayne Webb
Photography: Ray Lightfoot
See more: November 2007 **BRM**

Trackplan

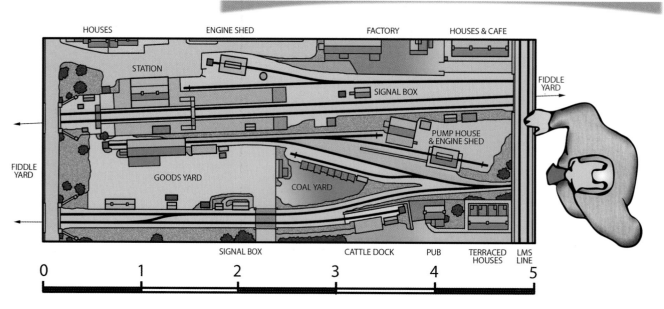

HOUSES   ENGINE SHED   FACTORY   HOUSES & CAFE

STATION

SIGNAL BOX

FIDDLE YARD

PUMP HOUSE & ENGINE SHED

FIDDLE YARD

GOODS YARD

COAL YARD

SIGNAL BOX   CATTLE DOCK   PUB   TERRACED HOUSES   LMS LINE

0   1   2   3   4   5

SHEPHERDS BUSH

Colin Cook chose a scale undergoing something of a renaissance to model his compact Great Western terminus.

Colin started railway modelling in the early 1960s, with Tri-ang TT equipment. When he became aware of the Three Millimetre Society, he joined it in 1968. It encouraged him to start scratch-building and its shop and various items was found to be a great help.

The trackplan used for his model of 'Shepherds Bush' came from the well used 'Minories' plan by Cyril Freezer, scaled down to 3mm:1ft using a track gauge of 12mm.

The scenic section of the layout is housed on two 6ft boards, allowing them to be loaded across the width of Colin's car, however, the fiddleyard board is slightly wider to accomodate the swing of the sector plate.

Track is hand-built from code 60 bullhead rail, soldered to PCB sleepers.

He'd hoped to make the fiddleyard exit a double track section, as with the Minories design, however a lack of room for points resulted in it being adapted to single track rather than remove all of the track.

Colin's collection of locomotives has been built over many years, either from scratch, kits or tinplate models. Consider the availability of stock before choosing a scale. ■

Pros

I Printed brick buildings make up for slow track-laying process. Guttering helps conceal joins between buildings
I TT can offer similar levels of detail to OO gauge using less space

Cons

I 'Minories' is a popular trackplan, but through overuse has become predictable. Adapting it to better suit your needs is a better option than copying it

Factfile

Layout name: Shepard's Bush
Scale/gauge: 3mm:1ft scale / TT gauge
Size: 6ft x 1ft 4in (plus fiddleyard)
Era/region: 1925-1935 GWR
Location: West London
Layout type: Fiddleyard to terminus
Owner: Colin Cook
See more: **BRM** Annual 2008

Trackplan

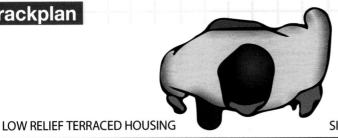

LOW RELIEF TERRACED HOUSING   SIGNAL BOX

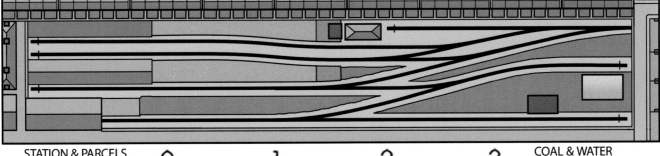

STATION & PARCELS   0   1   2   3   COAL & WATER

FLOCKBURGH

Fancy trying a different scale? Phil Parker did just that with his first essay in 3mm scale modelling.

After completing the build of the 'Hellingly Hospital railway' (see page 16) with his father, Brian, a new layout was on the cards. Building something different was a must - an 'off-beat' prototype and an unusual scale sounded like a good idea. As the rolling stock looked like it was available, 3mm beckoned.

With these two factors aside, Flockburgh is conventional. A small terminus in the BR steam era would be unremarkable in OO gauge. You could visit your local model shop and buy most of the stock off the shelf ready-to-run. Buildings from Hornby, track from Peco - most of the layout could be built in a weekend. The biggest decision for them was in the choice of track gauge to use. At the time, Phil was aware of two choices: 12mm gauge as used by Tri-ang, or 14.2mm,

the premier scale version of P4. There is a third - 13.5mm, but Phil wasn't aware about this at the time.

They found building the fiddleyard difficult - cassettes were considered, but in the end a traverser required less work.

It works on sliders from a filing cabinet. Alignement, electrical supply and locking is provided by a home-made bolt.

The track is soldered together using PCB sleepers and code 65 rail. Brian used 4mm:1ft scale plans, reduced to 3mm:1ft

Trackplan

STATION   ENGINE SHED   GOOD

0   1   2

BEACH   WATER   COAL YARD
             TANK

scale on a photocopier.

Considerable adjustment was required with the track to get locomotives and stock to perform properly. They learnt a lot about gauge widening on anything but a straight section of track. One of the benefits of PCB sleepers is that the rail can be unsoldered and adjusted to suit easily.

If you're moving to a new scale, consider building a test track. When the layout started, Phil and Brian weren't sure if the running problems were because of faulty rolling stock or poorly-laid track. Now that everything works, troublesome track is easier to identify.

The modelling book *The Art of Weathering* is recommended by Phil, but don't overdo the effects as they can look too much in 3mm scale.

Reflecting back on the project, Flockburgh is an amalgam of lots of different areas. It appeals and looks nice, but doesn't really represent any geographical location. Phil has tried to rectify this over the years. ■

Factfile

Layout name: Flockburgh
Scale/gauge: TT gauge
Size: 9ft x 1ft 4in
Era/region: BR terminus 1950s
Location: Fictitious
Layout type: Fiddleyard to station
Owner: Phil and Brian Parker
Photography: Ray Lightfoot
See more: April 2007 **BRM**

Pros

I The fast installation of the layout helps when exhibiting
I Popular with exhibition managers because of its size and quirky scale

Cons

I Compensation is recommended in 14.2mm gauge on any locomotive bigger than an 0-4-0 and track takes patience to build correctly

FIDDLE YARD

BANKFIELD ROAD

John Kneeshaw improved the original design of this O gauge layout purchase.

John discovered an advert for a nine foot long layout for sale, just 45 minutes from his house. He wanted a small O gauge layout that would appeal to the exhibition managers of smaller shows; and one that would be a lot easier to transport. He discussed the price and agreed to drive over and have a look. Not a very large sum of money changed hands and the layout was taken back home.

The original builder had developed a good design and a good scenic eye, but the more mundane things like how it fitted together, and how it ran, were less encouraging. The trackwork, which had looked alright in someone else's loft, proved to be problematical. Each of the tracks leading from the double slip in the centre of the layout had a dog-leg formation that he had to remove. Bankfield Road's track

plan is simple but effective. A sector plate in the fiddle yard leads the track under an overbridge and onto the visible part of the layout. This line leads into the small single platform station where there is a locomotive release turnout. The line from the locomotive release arrives at a double slip, then back to the fiddle yard sector plate. The first of the other two lines that run from the double slip travel past a small coal staith to the canal basin and into a 'down-at-heel' goods shed. The second runs under the overbridge and into a factory siding. ■

Pros

I A pre-built layout can be a quick way to get started, but be wary of the quality of workmanship
I Layouts are often sold for less than they're worth

Cons

I Always insist on a viewing with stock running on the layout.
I Most second-hand layouts will require remedial work or partial rebuilds

Factfile

Layout name: Bankfield Road
Scale/gauge: O gauge
Size: 9ft x 2ft
Era/region: 1940s LMS
Location: Fictitious
Layout type: Fiddleyard to dock sidings
Owner: John Kneeshaw
Photography: Paul Bason
See more: March 2013 **BRM**

Trackplan

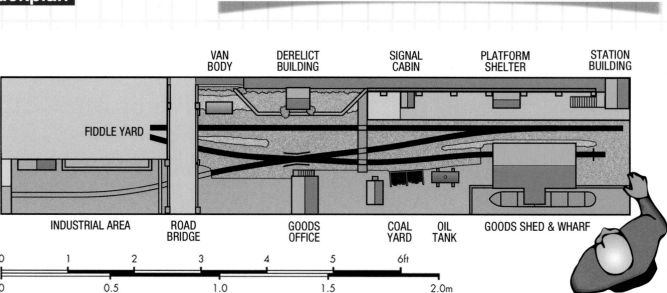

BLEAKHOUSE ROAD

Operating a layout single-handedly encouraged Tim Maddocks to include more than one focal point on his S&D-themed exhibition layout.

Keeping with his passion for all railway-related Somerset & Dorset things, he thought the Somerset Levels and the Highbridge branch of the S&D in particular offered scope for a new project. He had always preferred to model fictitious locations, albeit in the style of the prototype so as not to have to slavishly adhere to traffic patterns, rolling stock and operating restrictions of a real location.

The assumed background of an independant, local company allowed him to use certain non-S&D structures for the project, such as the McKensie & Holland signal box and the Eassie station building. The concoction of an invented history

called for a study of the real railways in the surrounding area and a reasonable knowledge of the geography and topography of the district.

Using a single operator for movements made Tim realise that the scenic section would need more than one focus of interest, hence the peat works and the South Polden Light Railway (SPLR) elements were created, together with the short section of operational narrow gauge peat tramway. ∎

Pros

I Extra focal points keep the eye busy between movements
I Lower canal basin with embankment creates photogenic viewpoints

Cons

I Juggling between the control of a narrow gauge line and the rest of the layout could prove problematic unless one of these systems is automated

Factfile

Layout name: Bleakhouse Road
Scale/gauge: 4mm:1ft / OO gauge
Size: 8ft x 1ft 10in
Era/region: British Railways (1959-1968)
Location: Somerset & Dorset
Layout type: Fiddleyard to fiddleyard
Owner: Tim Maddocks
Photography: Andy York
See more: April 2013 **BRM**

Trackplan

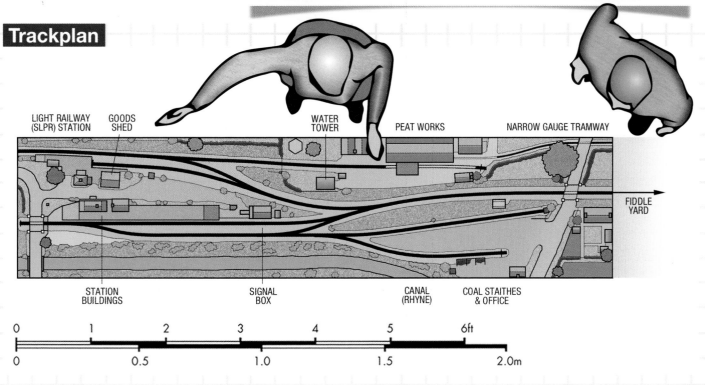

LIGHT RAILWAY (SLPR) STATION   GOODS SHED   WATER TOWER   PEAT WORKS   NARROW GAUGE TRAMWAY

FIDDLE YARD

STATION BUILDINGS   SIGNAL BOX   CANAL (RHYNE)   COAL STAITHES & OFFICE

0   1   2   3   4   5   6ft

0   0.5   1.0   1.5   2.0m

EAST ST. WHARF

Margaret Evans' creation depicts an EM gauge canal/railway interchange set somewhere in the Midlands.

After leaving Lincolnshire, Margaret lived in the Midlands for some years, and at the age of 15 her first job was in a steel stockholder's office overlooking a railway yard. From that an idea arose for a layout, set somewhere in the Midlands area. The period chosen was the start of Nationalisation onwards, based on a canal/railway Interchange.

'East St. Wharf' has two boards, each measuring 4ft x 2ft. Margaret had previously used trestles for support but found they were too bulky to transport, so used drop-in legs this time, a great space saving idea. Two legs support one board, with a crossed locking bar. The other board is supported on one set of legs in the centre and these are bolted together through alloy bushes which also align the tracks.

To transport the layout, two boards are bolted to end plates to keep them apart. This then forms a 4ft x 2ft x 1ft' 6in box. This time one end board has wheels fixed to it to enable it to be easily transferred to the exhibition hall from the car. ■

Factfile

Layout name: East St. Wharf
Scale/gauge: EM gauge
Size: 8ft x 2ft
Era/region: 1950s British Railways
Location: Midlands
Layout type: Cassettes to yard sidings
Owner: Margaret Evans
Photography: Tony Wright
See more: December 2006 **BRM**

Pros

I Lightweight layout that can be easily transported around exhibitions
I Raised retaining wall and houses to the rear add height

Cons

I Consider the costs of conversions and time required on locomotives and rolling stock if building an EM gauge layout.
I Hand-built track requires patience to build

Trackplan

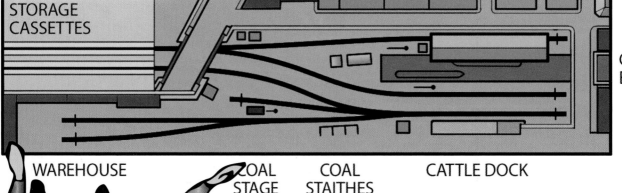

STORAGE CASSETTES

TERRACED HOUSES   PUB

CANAL BASIN

WAREHOUSE   COAL STAGE   COAL STAITHES   CATTLE DOCK

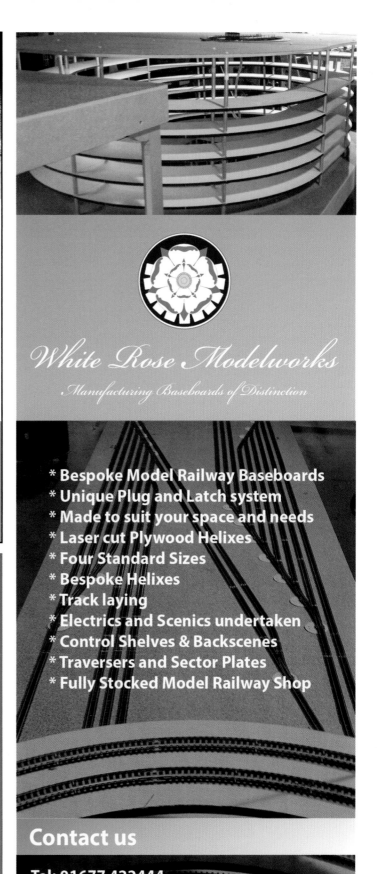

BILLINGBOROUGH

Graham Moorfoot's childhood memories played a great influence on his choice of location for a new 'back to basics' exhibition layout.

Having modelled North American HO for over 30 years, Graham decided to start a new layout project whilst on holiday in January 2012 and completed it in the May of that year. His choice to model Billingborough was entirely natural because he'd often ride the footplate of the locomotive on the daily pick-up goods hauled by a J6 locomotive.

He chose to model the location using the trackplan as it was in the 1950s and 1960s, but chose to compromise the scale of the site due to space restrictions in his layout room and problems with transportation – this was to be an exhibition layout.

Assembly of the boards takes place in minutes using alignment dowels to ensure alignment of tracks between boards, whilst toggle clasp fasteners save unbolting nuts underneath boards at the end of a show.

From the outset, Graham wanted the layout to be simple to operate, but also simple to maintain. A single DC hand-held controller with just three feeds to the layout ensures operation, whilst points and signals are operated manually using brass rods hidden underneath the boards. The level crossing even works, operated with manual worm and cog gear mechanisms.

'Billingborough' has a three-track turntable to turn trains without handling and can be incorporated into a larger permanent layout by adding extensions in modular form. ∎

Pros

❘ A great way to recreate childhood memories of a location much changed and share them with others
❘ More to this trackplan than meets the eye - a cattle dock, goods shed and coal yard can be shunted individually, whilst twin tracks through the station can be used effectively in an operating sequence

Cons

❘ Trackplans of real locations are designed to serve a function, not look good - choose your location wisely, some locations are more modellable than others
❘ Fiddleyards are required at both ends of the layouts to operate effectively

Factfile

Layout name: Billingborough
Scale/gauge: OO gauge
Size: 9ft x 2ft (plus fiddleyard)
Era/region: 1960s BR Eastern Region
Location: Billingborough
Layout type: Fiddleyard to through station
Owner: Graham Morfoot
Photography: Paul Bason
See more: July 2013 **BRM**

Trackplan

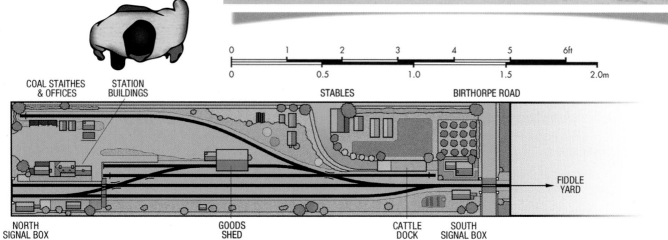

COAL STAITHES & OFFICES   STATION BUILDINGS   STABLES   BIRTHORPE ROAD

0   1   2   3   4   5   6ft
0   0.5   1.0   1.5   2.0m

FIDDLE YARD

NORTH SIGNAL BOX   GOODS SHED   CATTLE DOCK   SOUTH SIGNAL BOX

EAGLE LANE

Richard Coleman's OO gauge shunting layout is proof that small spaces needn't compromise levels of entertainment.

Eagle Lane is a freight yard based in the Wednesbury area of the industrial West Midlands in the 1985-1990 period. At this time, the area was still busy, with lots of freight terminals serving the appetite for metal products. Local freight trains would bring in wagons from Bescot or Washwood Heath to Wednesbury to then be sorted and delivered to Eagle Lane by a Class 08 shunter or mainline locomotive. The two main customers at Eagle Lane are Hammer Steel and Norton Metals. Owing to limited siding space, condemned wagons are pulled off the track by machine for breaking up.

Richard designed the layout on two boards – the scenic measuring 6ft x 15in, the fiddleyard 4ft x 15in. At home, the layout lives in his loft room and sits on two tables. Operating the layout takes place from the front and points are operated by piano wire push rods. Two sidings are fitted with isolated sections to assist shunting because operation is via 12V DC.

A simple loop allows trains to be 'run around' before being split into sections or shunted into sidings or the shed. ■

Factfile

Layout name: Eagle Lane
Scale/gauge: OO gauge
Size: 10ft x 1ft 3in
Era/region: BR 1985-1990
Location: West Midlands
Layout type: Fiddleyard to sidings
Owner: Richard Coleman
Photography: Paul Bason
See more: June 2013 **BRM**

Pros
I Use of half-relief cast resin buildings ideal if not confident with scratch-building
I Trackplan isn't linear and follows similar practice to many freight depots.
I Good use of surrounding space to create
I Layout is operated from the front at shows

Cons
I Consider adding animation to simple layouts like these to make the space work harder – a lit cutters torch, opening shed door or possibly rotating crane jib.

Trackplan

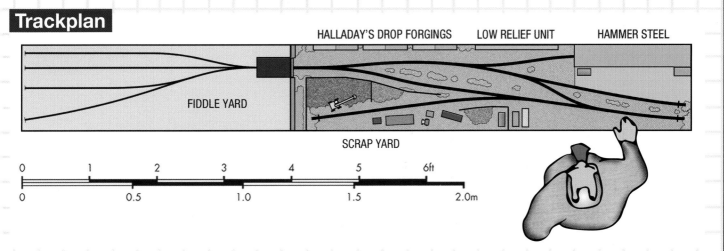

HALLADAY'S DROP FORGINGS   LOW RELIEF UNIT   HAMMER STEEL

FIDDLE YARD

SCRAP YARD

| 0 | 1 | 2 | 3 | 4 | 5 | 6ft |
| 0 | 0.5 | 1.0 | 1.5 | 2.0m |

OLDHAM KING ST.

Building a compelling minimum space plan to a budget can prove difficult when pushed for time, but this modern image layout ticks both boxes.

Factfile

Layout name: Oldham King Street
Scale/gauge: O gauge
Size: 8ft x 2ft
Era/region: 1980s - 2000s
Location: Fictitious
Layout type: Fiddle yard to terminus
Owner: David Hampson
See more: **MRM** Winter 2005

O riginally called 'Percy Street' and built by Ian Futers, 'Oldham King Steet' was later modified by David Hampson. The layout focuses more on entertaining the public with its rolling stock than architectural features. For this, rolling stock is fitted with DCC sound, lights and smoke units and occassionally a working crane is brought out to re-lift a wagon back onto the rails.

Space saving techniques are employed to their fullest. Two traditional single platforms aren't used, replaced instead with a single island platform in the station. The layout front is devoid of architectural features and the backscene is made of two layers - a retaining wall behind which low-relief buildings pose.

Just three points are used, creating two stub sidings at one end. In these areas wagons or locomotives can be parked and left to idle with sound. Colour light signals and bufferstop lights are other areas of interest, but the layout was designed to be quick to build and take to shows, so in the interests of saving time, complex architecture, a station building or signal box have been omitted. ■

Pros

I Quick to build
I Reduced track costs - only three points
I Easy to control by one person
I Can be set up at shows with speed

Cons

I Layout relies heavily on entertaining the public with operations
I stub sidings would benefit from extra length to display larger locomotives

> **'Oldham King Street' focuses more on entertaining the public with its rolling stock and operations than with its architectural features"**

> **Rolling stock is fitted with DCC sound, lights and smoke units. Occassionally a working crane is brought out to lift a wagon back onto the rails**"

Low Relief Industry

Wickes

Trackplan

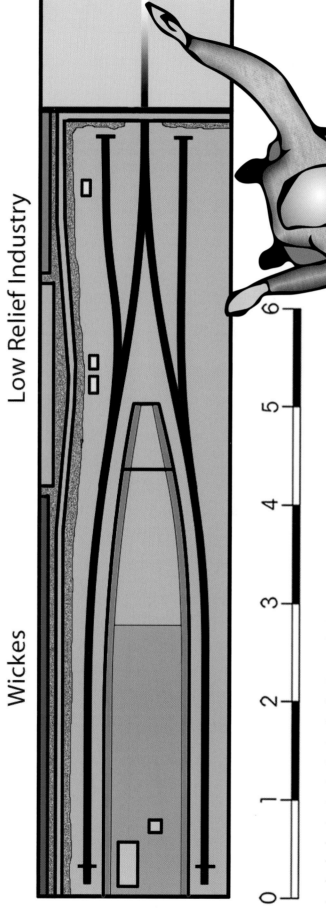

6

5

4

3

2

1

0

FISHERTON SARUM

Graham Muspratt's OO gauge Southern Railway shed is an adaptation of a real location, set just after nationalisation.

Taking a real location, using its buildings and their relationships with each other to create the spirit of that location, seemed a good idea for Graham Muspratt.

Using Salisbury as the inspiration for many of the buildings on 'Fisherton Sarum' was an obvious choice because he had a family connection.

One of the reasons for building a layout based on a shed in the first place was an opportunity to exhibit his increasing collection of Southern locomotives. On this layout, and to fit the available space he modelled the LSWR design style of shed but reduced it from ten roads to four and transposed it to the east with access from a kick-back arrangement rather than a fan of sidings which saves space.

Dominating the middle of the layout is the elevated coal stage and ramp that a short rake of loaded coal wagons are regularly pushed up by one of the shed's pilot engines.

He hopes many will find the theme instantly recognisable. Drawings of the London & South Western Railway designed buildings at Salisbury along with photographs were consulted to portray the location as an adaptation. To the rear of the layout, the mainline is kept busy for entertainment with passing expresses and goods trains, and a carriage siding beyond that is used to display passenger stock. ∎

Pros

▮ Using a real location as the basis for a trackplan saves time - if elements won't fit, replace, move or delete them to suit
▮ A shed layout is ideal if you've more locomotives than stock to display

Cons

▮ Considerable off-scene storage (not pictured) is required to accurately display the correct length of trains travelling between the West Country and London.
▮ DCC is highly recommended to effectively operate locomotives on shed - conversion costs from DC might be off-putting to some

Factfile

Layout name: Fisherton Sarum
Scale/gauge: OO gauge
Size: 8ft x 3ft
Era/region: Southern Region late-1940s
Location: Fictitious
Layout type: Fiddleyard to fiddleyard
Owner: Graham Muspratt
Photography: Paul Bason
See more: February 2012 **BRM**

Trackplan

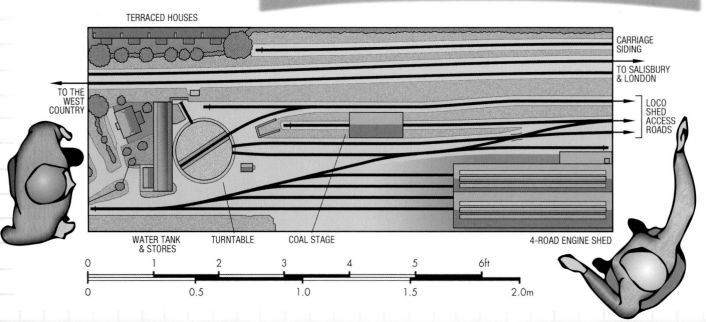

TERRACED HOUSES

CARRIAGE SIDING

TO SALISBURY & LONDON

TO THE WEST COUNTRY

LOCO SHED ACCESS ROADS

WATER TANK & STORES   TURNTABLE   COAL STAGE   4-ROAD ENGINE SHED

0   1   2   3   4   5   6ft

0   0.5   1.0   1.5   2.0m

GLENUIG

Recalling memories of youth spent on holiday in the Scottish Highlands, Gary Hinson constructed this fictitious West Highland branch.

After returning from one of his Scottish excursions, Gary had tried a little sketching to capture one of the wonderful Scottish Island scenes. On the rear of this trackplan he'd sketched a trackplan which was to become Glenuig.

The criteria of his design was - like for many exhibition layouts - that it had to be portable, fit in the family car, be set up and dismantled easily and fit in his workshop.

Over the years, Gary has tried most of the popular scales and he was impressed with the quality of OO gauge items now available. He'd calculated that using this scale would make his trackplan a snug fit for the room he had.

A four road turntable fiddle yard combined with Sprat & Winkle auto couplings avoids excessive handling of locomotives and stock on the layout. ■

Factfile

Layout name: Glenuig
Scale/gauge: 4mm:1ft / EM gauge
Size: 7ft x 1ft 6in (plus fiddleyard)
Era/region: 1970s / 1980s
Location: West Highlands
Layout type: Fiddleyard to terminus
Owner: Gary Hinson
Photography: Gary Hinson
See more: January 2013 **BRM**

Pros

I A field trip is useful to take measurements and photographs of a place you'd like to model - as was the case here
I Quayside wall, sea, backscene and sparse features recreate a remote atmosphere

Cons

I Track is built from C&L components - a lot of work, but worth the effort
I 500 mile journey to photograph backscene

Trackplan

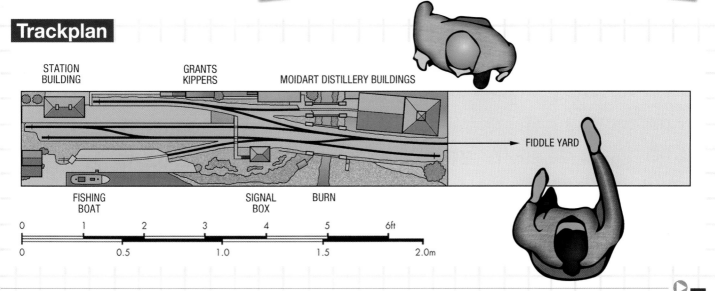

STATION BUILDING   GRANTS KIPPERS   MOIDART DISTILLERY BUILDINGS

FIDDLE YARD

FISHING BOAT   SIGNAL BOX   BURN

0   1   2   3   4   5   6ft

0   0.5   1.0   1.5   2.0m

HEMLOCK DOWN

John Worsley's layout based on the Culm Valley is packed with great ideas.

Hemlock Down was deliberately conceived as an exercise in building a layout of minimal length and weight. As such it's only 8ft 6in in length and can, if necessary, be assembled by one person. It's also small enough to be transported in an estate car as well as fitting entirely in one room, thereby greatly aiding its completion.

The station owes much to Hemyock on the Culm Valley line, although it has been altered in respect of the siding arrangements and by the removal of the creamery which was such a feature of Hemyock. However, it remains a small rural station in the light railway tradition, with buildings in the standardised style set by Arthur Paine for many light railways all over England. The real feature of the layout lies below the trackbed rather than above, in the

construction of the baseboards which are bult from 3mm and 6mm birch ply using a cellular box construction. Three longitudinal beams, 6in deep, support a series of profiled cross-members set at 6in intervals. Further weight was saved by 'skeletonising' parts. The result is a structure which is more reminiscent of the innards of an aeroplane wing - light enough to be easily picked up, yet is at least as stiff as a more traditional framed, flat-topped baseboard of significantly greater weight. ∎

Pros ✓

I Baseboard construction is often rushed with layout builds, but it's important to get right. Correcting mistakes later is almost impossible without consequences to scenery
I Sector plate kicking back underneath a hill to hide the fiddleyard is a great use of space
I Curved baseboards make the layout flow

Cons ✗

I The layout design creates the illusion of a quiet terminus because of its scenery - bear this in mind if 'scenically challenged'

Factfile

Layout name: Hemlock Down
Scale/gauge: EM gauge
Size: 8ft 6in x 2ft 8in (at widest point)
Era/region: 1930s GWR
Location: Devon
Layout type: Storage roads to terminus station
Owner: John Worsley
Photography: Ray Lightfoot
See more: August 2013 **BRM**

Trackplan

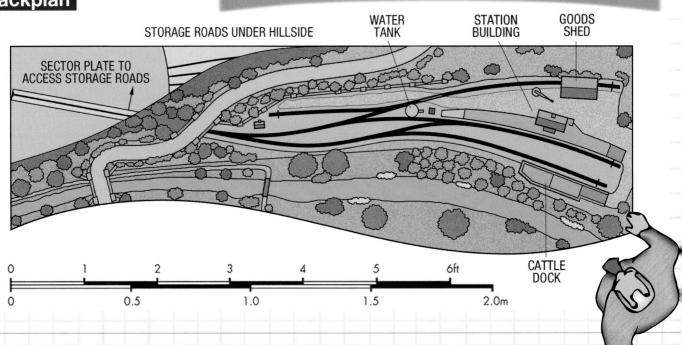

STORAGE ROADS UNDER HILLSIDE WATER TANK STATION BUILDING GOODS SHED

SECTOR PLATE TO ACCESS STORAGE ROADS

CATTLE DOCK

0   1   2   3   4   5   6ft

0   0.5   1.0   1.5   2.0m

BARNSTONEWORTH

Mid-way through an ongoing trackplan design, Pete Latham took a cycle ride through the Peak District which inspired this tiered layout.

For a number of years, Pete built N gauge shunting layouts, but thought it time for a change. One of his first inspirations came from the quality of DMUs available from Graham Farish and Dapol in recent years. He wanted a layout that would include a station - but which one to choose?

His initial intention was to base his layout on Shaw located on the Oldham loop - once double track, but now reduced to single in recent years. He drew plans , but a cycle ride into the Peak District changed everything when he discovered New Mills Central station.

He thought modelling the location would prove difficult because of the topography - the railway was built on a ledge carved into the hillside and then burrows under New Mills, then emerging from a tunnel onto a viaduct over the River Sett.

With just eight feet to spare, Pete knew he had to be selective - he copied the trackplan, station and viaduct, but decided to omit the town section.

Construction of the track is relatively simple using Peco code 55 for most areas with the exception of the hidden curves which use Peco code 80 and include four points. Although the trackplan appears to be a double track, it's effectively a loop. ∎

Pros

I   Large fiddleyard with room to accomodate 19 trains
I   N gauge is used to best effect when modelling a railway in a landscape
I   Return loop acting as fake double track mainline helps single operator when exhibiting

Cons
I   Prototype location features the River Goyt 100ft below the railway line and a hill rising 300ft above

Factfile
Layout name: Barnstoneworth
Scale/gauge: N gauge
Size: 8ft x 2ft
Era/region: 2000s Network Rail
Location: Peak District
Layout type: Continuous loop
Owner: Pete Latham
Photography: Richard Wilson
See more: July 2013 **BRM**

Trackplan

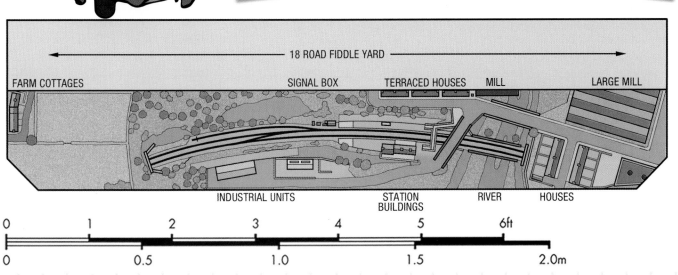

18 ROAD FIDDLE YARD

FARM COTTAGES   SIGNAL BOX   TERRACED HOUSES   MILL   LARGE MILL

INDUSTRIAL UNITS   STATION BUILDINGS   RIVER   HOUSES

0   1   2   3   4   5   6ft
0   0.5   1.0   1.5   2.0m

IMPERIAL YARD

Building a model railway to suit pre-existing baseboards can create design limitations, but it proved too tempting for Pete Latham to overlook.

Factfile

Layout name: Imperial Yard
Scale/gauge: N gauge
Size: 8ft x 14in to 2ft
Era/region: Network rail 2000s
Location: Fictitious
Layout type: Fiddleyard to yards
Owner: Pete Latham
Photography: Richard Wilson
See more: April 2013 **BRM**

Building 'Imperial Yard' was described by Pete Latham as a challenge. He was often told at exhibitons by visitors that they'd love to build a model railway, but hadn't the room. Two baseboards were donated to him with the challenge that he had to include as many features on them as possible - and not all of it track.

With only 14in to use in width, he settled for a terminus, and after a few designs, found he was able to accommodate four different shunting areas : steel, LPG, a wagon repair works and civil engineer's sidings. This plan was found to work, but didn't leave him with enough room for a fiddleyard, so he added a triangular piece of plywood to give a maximum width of 2ft.

To break the flat-world appearance, he raised the steel sidings by 1in in height above the rest and cut the baseboard to make a culvert. Whilst 'Imperial Yard' doesn't represent a real location, its flowing trackplan can't be faulted for its clever use of space - many rail-connected industrial sites follow a similar outline where space around a facility is at a premium. ∎

Pros

I Seep electromagnets used to uncouple wagons automatically
I Wagon repair shop off line passing civil engineers sidings is an excellent use of space

Cons

I DC control limits operation to two areas. DCC would allow more operators to get involved controlling locomotives on same sections

"Control of the layout is by KPC and All Components hand-held units fed by an All Components twin transformer. Both transformers give good shunting speed, smooth acceleration and deceleration"

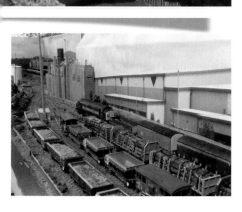

Trackplan

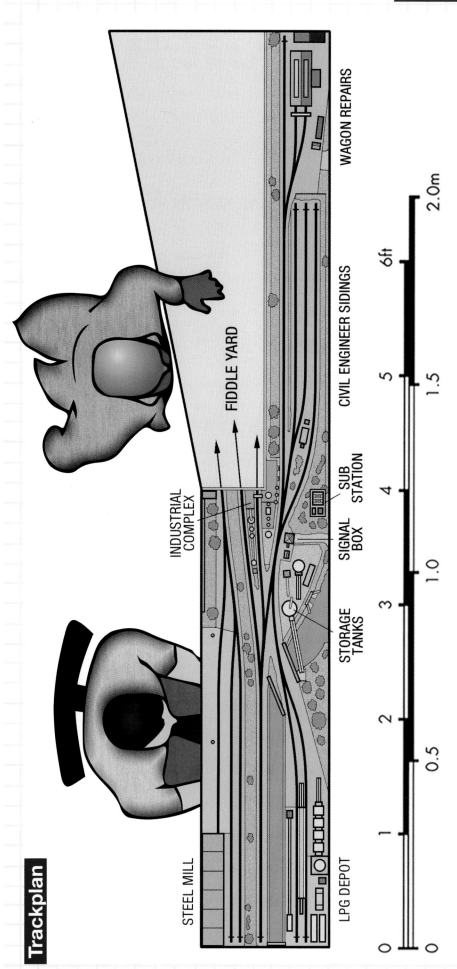

FIDDLE YARD

INDUSTRIAL COMPLEX

SUB STATION

SIGNAL BOX

STORAGE TANKS

CIVIL ENGINEER SIDINGS

WAGON REPAIRS

STEEL MILL

LPG DEPOT

0   0.5   1   1.5   2   3   4   5   6ft

0   0.5   1.0   1.5   2.0m

WISBECH AND UPWELL

This **BRM** project layout was designed as an acheivable project for beginners and made appearances at shows around the country.

Designed from the outset as a simple project that would cost little to build, the Wisbech and Upwell project layout was featured in **BRM** across issue in 2013.

Using nothing but a handheld controller, trains would represent the short workings that would take place across the tramway in the 1950s using Class 04 and J70 tram locomotives.

Just three points are used on the trackplan, none of which are controlled by motors - flicking them by hand when necessary is a quick and cheap solution. Problems were encountered with these during operation at its first exhibition outing because the electrical contact between the moving 'switch' rails and fixed 'stock' rails proved unreliable, leading to stuttering or stalling over points. The problem wasn't helped

either with the insulated point frogs and the short wheelbase locomotives with reduced number of pickups.

Changing point control to a 'wire in tube' method combined with a microswitch to provide a more reliable electrical contact was considered, but the layout was donated as a **BRM** prize before this took place.

Many visitors to the shows were surprised at how simple the layout was, but for a first layout, simplicity is often key. ∎

Pros

I Using a few 'ready-to-plant' houses, trees and hedges costs little to add to a 'bare shell' layout baseboard
I Little rolling stock is required

Cons

I Layouts with a simple trackplan require scenery to work harder as there's little to look at during quieter periods of operation.

Factfile

Layout name: Wisbech and Upwell
Scale/gauge: OO gauge
Size: 10ft x 1ft 6in
Era/region: 1950s BR Eastern Region
Location: East Anglia
Layout type: Fiddleyard to passing loop
Owner: **BRM**
Photography: **BRM**
See more: August 2013 **BRM**

Trackplan

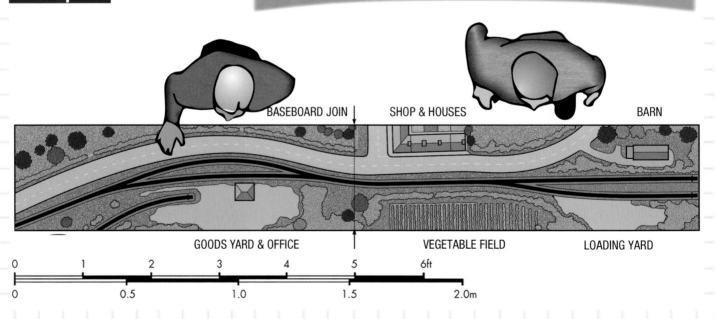

BASEBOARD JOIN   SHOP & HOUSES   BARN

GOODS YARD & OFFICE   VEGETABLE FIELD   LOADING YARD

| 0 | 1 | 2 | 3 | 4 | 5 | 6ft |

| 0 | 0.5 | 1.0 | 1.5 | 2.0m |

CORWENNA

Phil Waterfield's layout depicts the china clay-drying process in a fictitious Cornish location - a haven for small quirky locomotives.

With a spare room already fully occupied by his other layout 'Malham', Phil's layout 'Corwenna' would have to be portable and as small as possible.

Buildings are his favourite part of the model railway construction process, so these were designed and built before making the baseboards or laying track.

The baseboard had an initial footprint of 1500 x 500 mm which proved impractical when operating, so an increase in width and a 300mm extension enabled him to run a locomotive around seven wagons before returning.

Points and the wiring remain on the main board, which mean it can fit into a modest hatchback. The fiddle yard is a simple single track cassette 900 mm long, supported off the main board on a separate leg. ∎

Pros

▮ A single locomotive purchase often spurs the build of a new layout, as was the case here, with an 0-4-2T 'Beattie' Well tank
▮ Great architecture representing clay kilns, rarely seen on a model railway

Cons

▮ Variety of wagons and locomotives on the layout is very limited, so bear this in mind when choosing a prorotype - you'll need to factor in other elements to keep viewers entertained.

Factfile

Layout name: Corwenna
Scale/gauge: OO gauge
Size: 6ft 2in x 2ft 2in
Era/region: Southern Region 1956 - 1962
Location: Fictitious location in Cornwall
Layout type: Terminus to fiddle yard
Owner: Phil Waterfield
Photography: Andy York
See more: August 2017 **BRM**

Trackplan

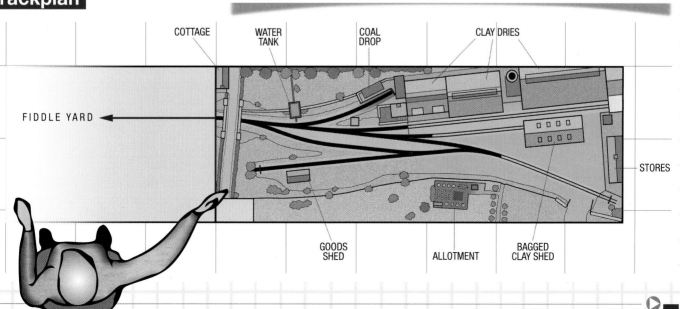

COTTAGE — WATER TANK — COAL DROP — CLAY DRIES

FIDDLE YARD ←

STORES

GOODS SHED — ALLOTMENT — BAGGED CLAY SHED

IMPROVE A DESIGN WITH FRESH IDEAS

Professional model railway planner, Paul Lunn, guides us through a selection of layout designs that he's adapted or improved to suit the end user.

No matter the level of a layout - beginner or advanced, fictional or not, I find it helpful to let prototype practice influence a design. You don't have to follow something slavishly, but it helps to have a semblance of reality to help guide your efforts and it's always improved the end result for me.

This layout, owned by a member of RMweb, made me think of the Liskeard to Looe line - a minimum space terminus at Liskeard, a semi-circuit of track dropping down grade under Liskeard Viaduct, carrying the line from Plymouth to Penzance and some pretty dramatic changes in topography, in all a gift of design inspiration.

As a designer I rarely work on paper straight away. Most of the initial thoughts are mind mapped in my head, to be transferred onto paper at a later time. So by

way of a quick journey through that process, Liskeard Viaduct becomes the aqueduct, the branch terminus is relocated along the rear half of the layout, track is spiralled from lower to upper levels giving extra running length and some interesting viewing angles and prototype topography applied to the available space, justified by the presence of a stream.

It's easy to see why the builder came to a standstill - there were problems, not in vision, but in some of the detail. 'Floating' aqueduct ends, an uninteresting lower level circuit, a flat baseboard with billiard table finish and a hole in the white backscene. I mention these, not as a criticism, but as the first step to finding a solution - identify what's wrong, unpick it and rebuild or replace for an improved end result.

I first met its builder at a show in 2013 and recall him patiently standing in the

BEFORE

background of one of my layout design and planning 'clinics'. Time is limited at these events and despite best efforts, he never managed to get time at the drawing board and his design issues went unresolved.

Ever aware of such lack of access, we exchanged contact details and what follows is an account of how we resolved the problems that had brought his layout to a grinding halt. It soon became clear that he was disappointed with the layout's

DMUs W51588/579 make their way down to Coombe Junction in August 1977.

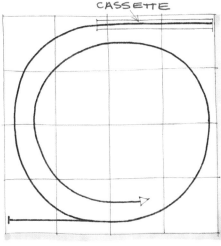

CASSETTE

LOWER LEVEL
TRACK DETAIL

EACH SQUARE
REPRESENTS
1'-00" FOR OO

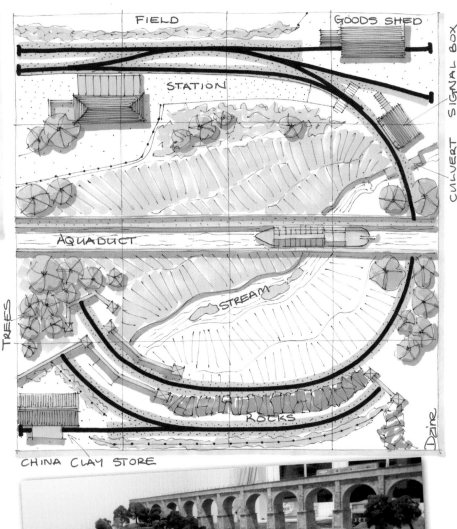

FIELD

GOODS SHED

SIGNAL BOX

STATION

CULVERT

AQUADUCT

TREES

STREAM

ROCKS

CHINA CLAY STORE

appearance and operating potential and whilst there were issues to be addressed, he glossed over what was his superbly spectacular and dramatic idea. 'Wow', I thought, unlike anything else for OO gauge – and on such a small baseboard. In every respect it was a concept layout, something that flies in the face of textbook suggestions, and therefore likely to cause a stir.

My only real concern was related to track gradient, in terms of appearance and in respect of the necessary clearance between non-scenic sidings and the terminus station. During the course of construction, Ian checked grades and tested individual items of rolling stock and was successful with a single railcar pulling one coach and a Class 08 with two or three wagons.

All that remained was to apply what we'd identified, some parts by trial and error, others just dropped into place with hardly any effort. What became apparent during this process was our joint capacity to share ideas, question the reasoning behind a particular thought and move the design collectively forward. Watching his progression was a highlight for me, looking forward to his photographic feedback as work progressed. There's still a bit to do, but you can't fail to see Ian's outstanding work, and his progression from the layout that once languished, for a year, unfinished in his loft to its current state. ∎

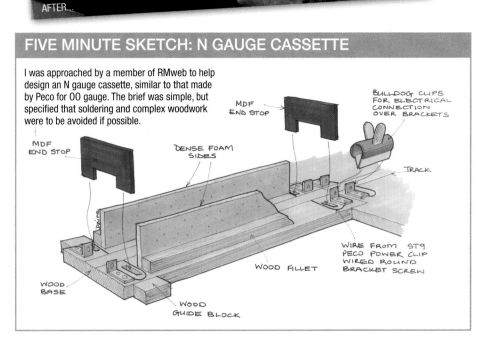

AFTER...

FIVE MINUTE SKETCH: N GAUGE CASSETTE

I was approached by a member of RMweb to help design an N gauge cassette, similar to that made by Peco for OO gauge. The brief was simple, but specified that soldering and complex woodwork were to be avoided if possible.

MDF
END STOP

BULLDOG CLIPS
FOR ELECTRICAL
CONNECTION
OVER BRACKETS

MDF
END STOP

DENSE FOAM
SIDES

TRACK

WIRE FROM ST9
PECO POWER CLIP
WIRED ROUND
BRACKET SCREW

WOOD
BASE

WOOD FILLET

WOOD
GUIDE BLOCK

CASE STUDY

Prototype research

There are two key ways of gaining legitimate access to Hope Works; either apply to visit or go on one of the occasional open days. During Blue Circle ownership staff were always happy to help and I have no reason to believe Lafarge would be any different. Once inside you have close-up access to a wonderful array of industrial images. Please note these photographs from August 1993 pre-date the recent modernisation programme. When planning a layout, you might need to gain access to a non-public site.

I've been undertaking surveys of active and disused railway lines from as far back as I can remember, partly for interest sake, but mainly as a resource to be filed for future use in my work as an author. These consist largely of taking photographs, notes and sometimes measurements of relevant stock or buildings. The breadth of recording varies from a few key details to an in-depth account, with most complete records usually reflecting my own interest. Those familiar with my work will be aware of the favourites; British Oak Coal Disposal Point, the Clayton West Branch, the ex-Cambrian and

so on. I never randomly turn up at a location without in-depth preparation, so as to make best use of all available resources.

Earliest research examples, for a 1970s operational route, show timetables cross-referenced to maps, so I could be at different vantage points along a route to coincide with passing trains. I'd allow enough time to travel between each location, test out possible photographic compositions and make notes. The longest gap, nearest mid-day, between trains would provide space for lunch and anything missed would be factored into the return trip. Whilst this process was not so important for easy to revisit prototypes near home, it became essential practice for those distant, one-time only, visits.

I still use a similar process nowadays, albeit more refined, and want to share with you the core features of my working practice to aid your own research efforts. For the purpose of this exercise I have chosen, the near to home main line and branch junction at Earles Sidings to Hope Cement Works.

PRE-VISIT CHECKLIST

- Assess rail route and all public access points; road intersections, the course of useful footpaths, nearby elevated topography or accessible buildings for possible photographic vantage points
- Refer to freight train timetables (Freightmaster, Realtime Trains) or local railway knowledge for incoming/outgoing main line train details. Much is now available on the internet through sites such as Realtime Trains.
- Talk to local staff/railway enthusiasts for internal operational detail. Much is also available on the internet
- Analyse all of the above to identify best route; with parking spots for road access, distances on foot and roughness of terrain. Factor in the time it takes to get from one location to another and identify the best location for all photography, bearing in mind angles, lack of access and position of the sun, preferably behind the camera for what I call reference shots.

This detailed image was part of a pamphlet given during my visit and holds a wealth of transferable modelling information, particularly in respect of this aerial view of the works trackplan and associated buildings. Elsewhere, the contents document the whole process of on-site cement making.

1. Raw materials store
2. Blending silos
3. Preheater building
4. Rotary kilns
5. Electrostatic precipitators
6. Clinker store
7. Cement millhouse
8. Auto loader building
9. Bulk cement storage silos
10. Coal discharge point
11. Coal stockpile

There's always a chance, particularly at a site like Hope, of stumbling over a wonderful cameo, ideal in its unusual detail. There's a potential micro-layout here and an opportunity for large scale shunting with a radio-controlled 'tractor'.

I cannot stress the importance of documenting all you see; sketches, written notes cross-referenced with photographs and detail everything. It's amazing how your memory can play tricks over time - beware!

Manipulating track components

In the past I've looked at constructing more realistically-spaced and interestingly-shaped passing loops based around the Peco Setrack or Hornby 'Y' point and the short second radius curve. I want to take that formation further and include it into a complete layout design, adding other factors not normally associated with rigid track starter-type layout plans. The prototype railway weaves around, in, out and through the natural landscape and has no baseboard edge. In this sense it's organic with very few sections of truly straight track. Clearly you can't do all of this on a model layout, but off-setting the entire track formation, not parallel to the baseboard edge, goes some way to creating a sense of realism. Furthermore - and also similar to reality - you'll have no sausage-like embankments filling the parallel voids between track and baseboard edge. You can clearly see the realistic benefit of reduced track spacing in the station loop, reverting to

wider spacing for the locomotive shed and goods siding. By contrast, on the opposite side of the layout, I've increased track centres, greater than the norm, for rigid geometry track, to accommodate a signalbox within the confines of the loop. Note also on this half of the layout how both curved corners are not the usual prescribed quarter circle, all part of improving visual realism.

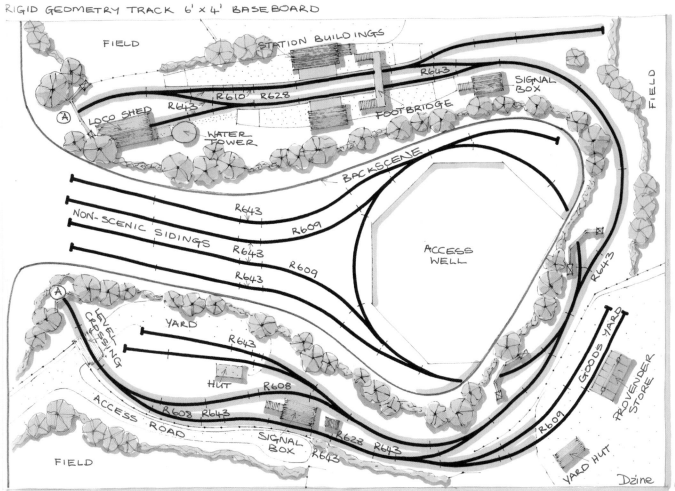

PYSTYLL-GRAIG-DDU

John and Owen Gibbon's minimum space O gauge layout depicts a colliery line on the Taff Vale Railway.

John and Owen Gibbon say to those put off by the size of O gauge, that they needn't worry. They still believe you can build a layout that is interesting to operate and attracts the attention of the public at shows.

The criteria for the layout was made based on the size they could get into a car, as well as the stock required to run it and their overnight bags. This limited the overall length of the scenic section to 9ft, with a width of 22in, with the height set at 38in which they find convenient to operate at. An additional 4ft x 1ft fiddle yard board gives a total overall length of 13ft.

The railway company they decided upon was the Taff Vale because they have numerous items of rolling stock and locomotives to be able to satisfy their needs at a show.

> "To accommodate these manoeuvres, there's a platform face, goods loading dock, small goods yard and reception road for coal wagons"

Trackplan

STATION BUILDING   BEAM ENGINE   ENGINE HOUSE   PIT HEAD GEAR

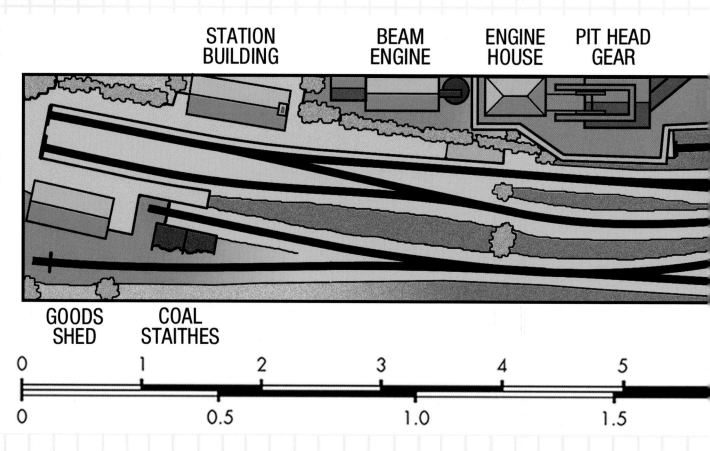

GOODS SHED   COAL STAITHES

```
0        1        2        3        4        5
0            0.5           1.0          1.5
```

The baseboards are connected by dowels from the EM Gauge Society for alignment, with case catches on the outside of the boards to lock them together. This makes for a quick assembly and knockdown at shows. The lighting gantry is made of timber with fluorescent lighting units in each half, allows it to be folded for transportation, these just slot onto the main baseboards, with no clamping or bolting required.

The fiddle yard board where all the service to the layout is made is a flat clear area where cartridge loading of the trains is made.

The trackwork was drawn out on the baseboards to see what could be acheived in such a small space, it had to be interesting for both operator and viewer and as can be seen from the trackplan, there are a number of moves required for each train that arrives. This ranges from passenger traffic with various attached vehicles, goods trains which require the odd wagon or two to be removed and replaced, to the mineral traffic, in this case coal, where empties arrive and loaded wagons depart.

To accommodate all these manoeuvres, there is a platform face, goods loading dock, small goods yard and basic reception road for empty/full coal wagons. A small screens area allows the empty coal wagons to be propelled and filled.

Trackwork was drawn out on the baseboards with the cork underlay being stuck to the board with double-sided tape.

Timber sleepers of scale thickness and length were cut from sheets of timber available at most model shops, for both the plain track and pointwork and positioned on the cork, again with double-sided tape.

Some time saving was saved by the use of ready machined blades and noses and the appropriate chairs for the bullhead rail purchased from C&L.

John and Owen decided from the outset that all the pointwork was to be operated by motors/solenoids, but they were all to be accessible at the rear of the boards. This allows for manual operation to keep things running or replacement without getting on hands and knees under the boards to change them in the unlikely event of failure. ■

Factfile

Layout name: Pystyll Graig Ddu
Scale/gauge: O gauge
Size: 9ft x 1ft 9in
Era/region: 1910-1920
Location: Fictitious (Taff Vale Railway)
Layout type: Fiddleyard to colliery
Owner: John and Owen Gibbon
Photography: Tony Wright
See more: BRM Annual 2013

Pros

I Freight and passenger operations mingle keeping the public guessing
I Wagon loading creates a visual event
I Demonstrates what can be acheived in O

Cons

I Scratch-built or kit-built stock required due to lack of RTR items
I If still short on space, consider removing 1ft from right of layout

SCREENS

FIDDLE YARD

SIGNAL BOX

2.0m

BOTTRILL STREET YARD

Nigel Adams built his second O gauge compact layout using just two points.

Factfile

Layout name: Bottrill Street Yard
Scale/gauge: O gauge
Size: 8ft x 2ft tapering to 1ft
Era/region: 1950s/'60s
Location: Fictitious
Layout type: Cassette to repair sheds
Owner: Nigel Adams
Photography: Tony Wright **BRM**
See more: February 2004 **BRM**

Building an interesting layout to fit a pre-built baseboard isn't recommended, but that's how Nigel's 'Bottrill Street Yard' came into being.

Before putting the boards together he started planning a possible layout design on lining paper using two Peco points and some track. Eventually he devised the plan shown opposite. Despite its simplicity, Nigel says it's enjoyable to operate because he likes smaller layouts, especially those with locomotive sheds or which require shunting. This layout allows him to combine both and can be used for three sequenced timetables as follows:

■ Both sheds are used a mixture of steam and diesel locomotives or one shed for diesels, the other for steam.

■ One shed is used for locomotives, the other as a wagon repair works.

■ Both sheds are used for wagon repairs

Two spirit levels bought in a DIY store are fitted to each baseboard, making it easy to see if the floor is level when setting up at exhibitions. The baseboards are joined by two nuts and bolts through the framework ends and also by hinges at the front and the rear with removable pins to give the same alignment each time the layout is moved and set up again.

Most of the scenery on 'Bottrill Street Yard' is added detail - an aspect of the hobby which Nigel really enjoys, so much so, that he added two boards to the layout front which are devoid of track. One is an excuse to display some of his models of vintage coaches, buses and cars. For 28 years he worked in the car industry and, at one stage, started to collect models of the vehicles for which he had prepared estimates or bought components. It became clear that this was going to create storage problems, so the idea was abandoned.

The two sheds seen on the layout are low-relief because of the narrowness of the board and the consequent design of the layout. Other parts of the two Heljan kits he used are now used as low-relief structures along the end and rear. A 'Pikestuff' kit by Rix Products was used to make a low-relief building on the second board. The other main building seen on the layout is the overhead signal cabin. In terms of its size, Nigel thinks it's 'over the top', but it effectively hides the exit to the cassettes and he likes it. If he needs to justify it, he says that it controls the main line which can't be seen. The baseboards join is covered by a Heljan removable footbridge. ■

> " I like layouts that include locomotive sheds. However, I'm not against some shunting and this new layout allows me to do both"

Pros

I Minimum space layout, ideal for many new O gauge RTR locomotives now available
I Use of just two points keeps costs low
I Little rolling stock required - good option for a first layout if starting in the scale

Cons

I Limited operational possibilities
I Repetition might become tiresome

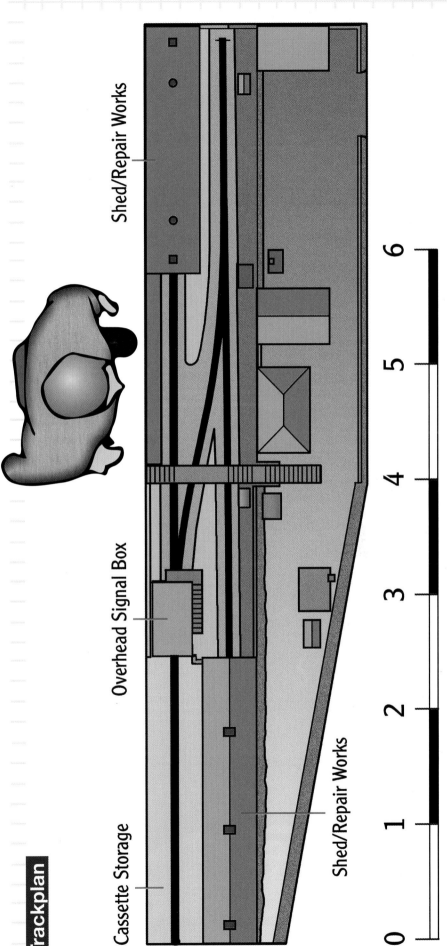

O
GAUGE

Trackplan

Shed/Repair Works

Overhead Signal Box

Cassette Storage

Shed/Repair Works

0 1 2 3 4 5 6

BLUE IS THE COLOUR

Following exhibition experience with another N gauge layout, Norman Jones built this layout to meet his future needs and expectations.

Blue is the Colour is a semi-rural model railway which can be extended with a wing to give a greater variety of rolling stock. It was Norman's first N gauge layout who was looking to build something he could take on the exhibition circuit, but also fit into a smaller home in the future. It also had to fit in his car - exhibition managers have to maintain an eye on expenses.

The layout measures 8ft x 2ft 6in, the main board being in two parts for transportation purposes. The wing has been constructed measuring 4ft x 1ft to enable greater stock to be used when on tour. The wing fits at right angles to the main board, allowing enough operating space in tight exhibition halls.

Peco Code 80 track has been used throughout, with medium radius turnouts and a generous track radii on the return loops prevents limitations on the stock that can be operated.

The layout is stored in a walk-in wardrobe when not touring exhibitions or being operated in the garage over the summer. ∎

Pros

I Building a smaller layout is a way of future-proofing a potential house downsize
I Scenery gives the layout two identities - the Scottish Lowlands and Welsh Marshes

Cons

I Difficulty in sourcing suitable road vehicles for this era and scale
I It took Norman three and a half years to build - be wary of timescales on projects

Factfile

Layout name: Blue is the Colour
Scale/gauge: N gauge
Size: 8ft x 2ft 6in (+ 4ft x 1ft for shows)
Era/region: 1975 - 1983
Layout type: Continuous loop
Owner: Norman Jones
Photography: Andy York
See more: Jan 2014 **BRM**

Trackplan

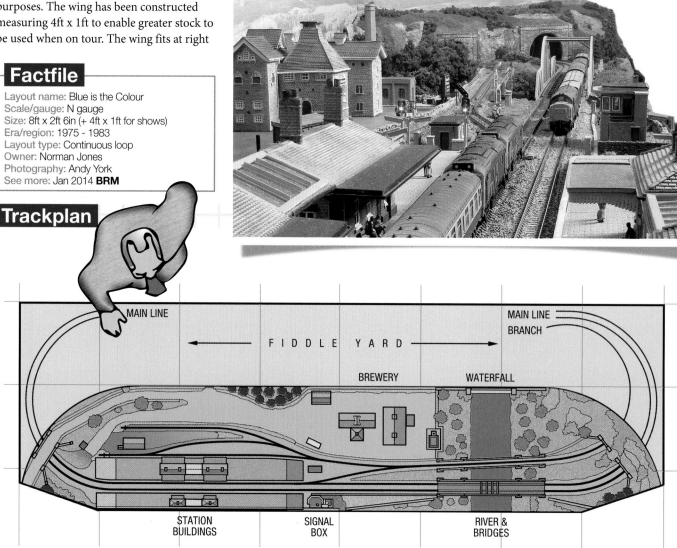

MAIN LINE

MAIN LINE
BRANCH

← F I D D L E   Y A R D →

BREWERY

WATERFALL

STATION
BUILDINGS

SIGNAL
BOX

RIVER &
BRIDGES

OO GAUGE

CROSS NESS

For the basis of his first OO gauge layout, Andrew Knights chose to model a compact third-rail terminus based in suburban Kent.

Wanting a layout to display an ever-growing collection of Electric Multiple Units (EMUs), Andrew built a small station terminus featuring a bay platform - the preserve of the Abbey Wood shuttle. Sometimes it hosts a visiting Motor Luggage Van (MLV) - a rare visitor to the station, but more often permanent way vehicles are stored.

The main platform can cope with over five coaches for London-bound trains. Adjacent to the station is a two-car carriage servicing platform. The rest of the track featured relates to the permanent way depot. A run-round loop and short sidings help sort stock before it's despatched elsewhere. Outside the depot building is a short length of inset track which marks the site of the old goods shed, demolished when the new depot building was constructed. The main yard for the depot is situated behind these buildings. ■

Pros

l Magnetic couplings are used to help couple models together quickly and without needing to intervene
l EMUs can be moved to the cleaning area occasionally to change working routes

Cons

l Modelling third-rail lines requires careful positionning of track and third rails

Factfile

Layout name: Cross Ness
Scale/gauge: OO gauge
Size: 6ft 6in x 1ft
Era/region: BR 1980s
Location: Kent
Layout type: Fiddleyard to terminus and sidings
Owner: Andrew Knights
Photography: Paul Bason
See more: September 2013 **BRM**

Trackplan

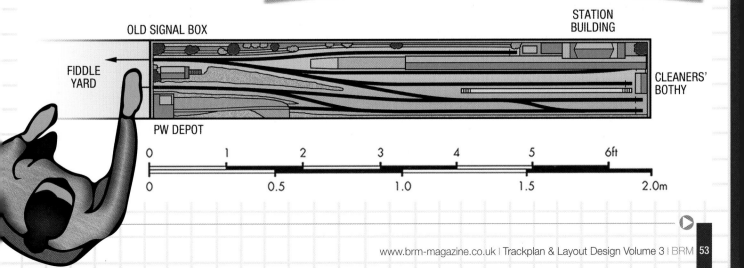

OLD SIGNAL BOX

STATION BUILDING

FIDDLE YARD

CLEANERS' BOTHY

PW DEPOT

| 0 | 1 | 2 | 3 | 4 | 5 | 6ft |

| 0 | 0.5 | 1.0 | 1.5 | 2.0m |

WOODSIDE MPD

Richard King describes the construction of his OO gauge layout, helped by fellow members from his club, Ilkeston Woodside MRC.

Woodside Lane isn't based on a particular location or period of operation, allowing Richard and a few members of his club the flexibility to use stock from all regions of British Rail - although there's a leaning towards the London Midland and Western regions from the 1970s to mid-80s.

During an operating session, stock from different eras is used with care to progressively blend into each era. Generally, locomotives arriving on shed travel directly to either of the two fuelling roads before moving around for stabling. Tank wagons are tripped on and off the depot as required.

A cassette system in the fiddle yard helps to swap locomotives, minimising handling and reduces the risk of damage to stock.

The layout was initially built to run a large ageing fleet of models, but these were all sold using the proceeds to buy more up-to-date diesels with extra detail.

Richard admits that 'Woodside Lane' has been an enjoyable project because its completion was achieved in a short time - it proved to be a refreshing diversion away from the clubs main project. The club now had somewhere to test new locomotives and rolling stock, serving its original purpose as a simple test track. Upgrading the layout to DCC was being considered at the time. ■

Pros

I Proprietry scenery helped completion of the layout for its first exhibition deadline
I The layout's foundations were recycled from a previous test track to keep costs low

Cons

I Second hand points from a previous layout were a false economy because of damaged point blades
I Layout activity is largely one-ended

Factfile

Layout name: Woodside Lane MPD
Scale/gauge: OO gauge
Size: 8ft x 2ft
Era/region: BR 1970s / 1980s
Location: London Midland / Western Region
Layout type: Fiddleyard cassettes to MPD
Owner: Richard King
Photography: Tony Wright **BRM**
See more: February 2011 **BRM**

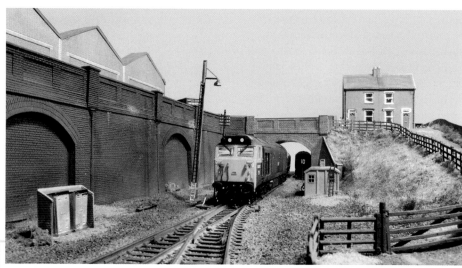

Trackplan

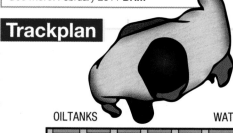

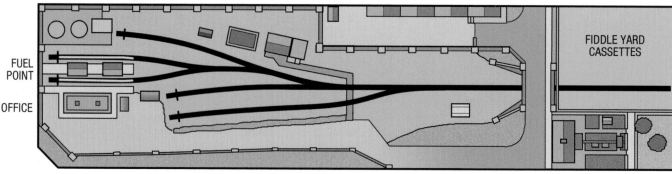

OILTANKS   WATER TOWER & OFFICE   FACTORY

FUEL POINT

OFFICE

FIDDLE YARD CASSETTES

HOUSE & GARDEN

0   1   2   3   4   5   6ft

0   0.5   1.0   1.5   2.0m

OO GAUGE

HARBOURNE

Shaun Greet's blue diesel era layout is a twist on the popular Great Western branch line terminus.

Having built three large continuous loop layouts, Shaun wanted his next layout to be more demanding in terms of operation rather than leave trains to run in circles. A compact layout was chosen to tax his brain – effectively a shunting puzzle in a limited space. Measuring 6ft x 1ft 6in was a requirement rather than a choice as the layout had to fit on the coffee table in his living room when assembled.

For Shaun, the level of detail on RTR steam locomotives was found to be more of a hindrance than a blessing at exhibitions because of damage, so he chose diesel locomotives, setting the layout in the 1968-1972 period, avoiding TOPS.

His trackplan needed to provide as much operational interest as possible without looking overcrowded and was interested in the end of the Beeching era when the railway was in a run-down state. He liked the idea of a railway in a run-down state, fighting to hang on to survive because of its atmosphere which appealed to him more than gleaming express trains running up and down well-kept lines. ∎

Pros

▎ Branch line passenger terminus with plenty of opportunity for goods traffic
▎ Traditional road bridge ahead of fiddleyard substituted for sector plate behind bushes
▎ Single locomotive operation avoids isolation sections

Cons

▎ Fiddleyard design found difficult to operate with its complex pointwork – cassettes or modules would be easier with short trains

Factfile

Layout name: Harbourne
Scale/gauge: OO gauge
Size: 6ft x 1ft 6in
Era/region: 1960s/1970s pre-TOPS
Location: Western Region
Layout type: Traverser to sector plate
Owner: Shaun Greet
Photography: Mike Wade
See more: June 2010 **BRM**

Trackplan

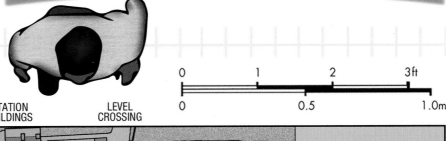

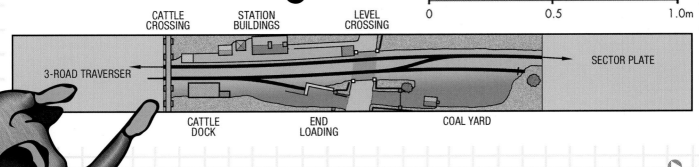

CATTLE CROSSING   STATION BUILDINGS   LEVEL CROSSING

3-ROAD TRAVERSER

SECTOR PLATE

CATTLE DOCK   END LOADING   COAL YARD

0   1   2   3ft
0   0.5   1.0m

SNEYD SIDINGS

Designed as a simple home layout, potential was seen in John Hill's railway/canal interchange scene as it hit the exhibition circuit.

Sneyd Sidings is an imaginary location to the South of the Cannock Chase coal field in the vicinity of Bloxwich and portrays a railway/canal interchange basin, typical of many found on the Birmingham Canal Navigation during the 1950s and '60s. In this imaginary location, local trade has expanded beyond coal traffic to include facilities for general goods and local passenger trains.

Forming a scenic break at the fiddleyard end, the abandoned track bed of the Cheslyn Hay Tramroad, here depicted in narrow gauge, crosses the standard gauge lines on a bridge.

John was a raw beginner to the hobby, never having built, landscaped or populated a layout. The amount of space he had was determined by the longest wall in a room – a chimney breast reduced the width of his fiddleyard and it is from here that he controls the layout.

He devised a trackplan using computer software that is an out-and-back, but gives the impression of a 'through' line. Beyond the station, the track is reduced to a single line which continues over a level crossing and into the backscene. Remnants of the track form a headshunt for a parcels facility before stopping short of the level crossing.

The all-important canal basin is short, barely a boat in length at a scale 72ft, that disappears under a Hornby Skaledale canal bridge forming a scenic break. A short siding off the station approach acts as a shed for the station shunter and includes coal and watering facilities for passing locomotives. Another area of activity is around Sneyd goods depot, where a covered bay and open dock with cranage are located. ■

Factfile

Layout name: Sneyd Sidings
Scale/gauge: OO gauge
Size: 6ft x 2ft (plus fiddleyard)
Era/region: West Midlands 1950s
Location: Fictitious
Layout type: Fiddleyard to terminus
Owner: John Hill
Photography: Tony Wright
See more: June 2009 **BRM**

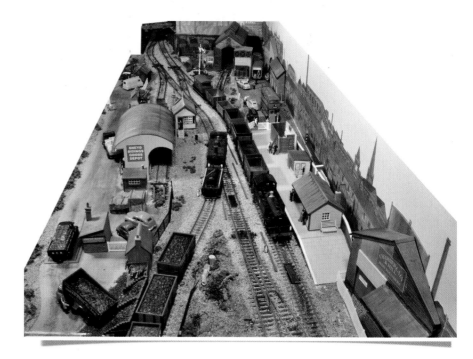

Trackplan

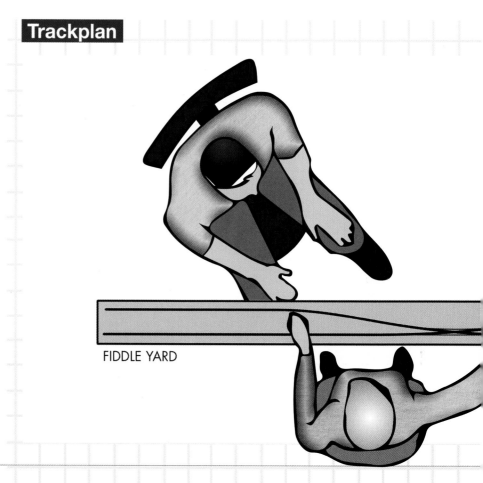

FIDDLE YARD

Pros

| Trackplan printed and glued to baseboards with spraymount ensures everything fits before fixing track
| Water level of canal is at baseboard height, surrounding terrain being 'built up'
| Good use of CAD to draw trackplan and design card buildings
| Double slip to fiddleyard increases storage space whilst allowing change over of tracks

Cons

| Ready to plant buildings still require additional painting to look their best
| Spring-loaded uncoupling ramps proved problematic when making contact with underside detail on locomotives

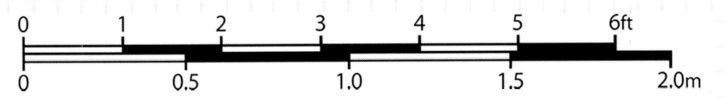

0   1   2   3   4   5   6ft

0   0.5   1.0   1.5   2.0m

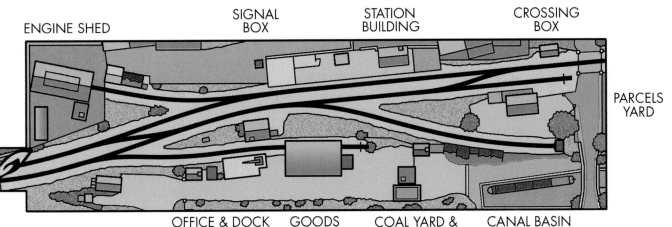

ENGINE SHED   SIGNAL BOX   STATION BUILDING   CROSSING BOX

PARCELS YARD

OFFICE & DOCK   GOODS SHED   COAL YARD & WEIGHBRIDGE   CANAL BASIN

STAMFORD & ESSENDINE

BRM's trackplan illustrator, Ian Wilson, offers a selection of trackplans in three scales based around a Great Northern Branch Line.

The Stamford & Essendine branch was the subject of my college thesis in 1969, and formed the base from which I developed the Prototype Models range of cardboard construction kits. Stamford East Signal Box in N gauge was the first kit and OO and O gauge versions were then produced, followed by models of Stamford Engine Shed in OO and O gauge. It was the start of a life-long interest in the branch and over the years I've devised lots of schemes for modelling the line, some of which are presented here.

Inside the train shed at the East Station a C12 4-4-2T has just arrived with the train from Essendine. Note the 6-wheel brake van next to the engine – this and a brake composite coach were the usual stock for branch trains. M N BLAND

STAMFORD AND ESSENDINE: back story

When the Great Northern Railway was building its line to the North of England in 1851 it was planned that the line should pass through Stamford, an important town on the A1 - the traditional coaching route from London to York and beyond. This would have meant that the line would pass for a short distance through the grounds of Burghley House. The owner of Burghley, the Marquess of Exeter, wasn't particularly impressed with the idea - so Stamford didn't get a main line connection to London. Exeter lived long enough to regret his lack of foresight and didn't oppose the coming of the Midland Railway's branch from Leicester to Peterborough in the early 1850s. The people of Stamford quickly realised the advantages of rail travel and aspired to higher things. What they wanted was a through train to London, so it was decided that a line should be built to connect with the Great Northern main line four miles to the east of the town. The leader in this movement was The Marquis of Exeter and so the Stamford and Essendine Railway Company came into being. Construction began in 1855, but progress was

ragged, and the line didn't open until November 1856. The hopes of a through train to London disappeared because the branch reached the main line at Essendine facing north rather than south to London - as did the other branch at Essendine from the town of Bourne. The station site at Stamford was limited on one side by the Midland line to Peterborough and on the other by the River Welland, making it compact - perfect for modelling!

The station was originally built to accommodate trains to Essendine only, but from 1867 until 1929 trains also ran to Wansford on the Rugby to Peterborough line of the LNWR (now home to the Nene Valley Railway). Although provision was made for double track over bridges, the line was single tracked except for the section between Stamford East and the Martin's Cultivators works. This section was operated as two single track lines, with one the running line and the other an industrial siding known as Priory Siding, which also served Priory Lime Works, the Lister Blackstone agricultural machinery works and a petrol and oil wharf.

All trains to Essendine called at the intermediate station of Ryhall and Belmesthorpe, a sleepy halt with only a single goods siding and a level crossing. Trains then continued to the main line connection at Essendine, running into the down slow line on the station's island

platform. The crew would pass the single line token to the stationmaster, and after taking water next to the North Signal Box would run round the train ready for return to Stamford.

The station closed in March 1957, trains then running to Essendine from Stamford Town station until the last train - hauled by N5 0-6-2T No. 69292 - travelled the line on June 15th 1959. The train left Stamford in a cloud of steam with its whistle blowing and detonators exploding on the line.

MODELLING STAMFORD & ESSENDINE

There are four main structures to consider when planning a model of Stamford East - the Station Building, the Goods Shed, the ex-GNR Signal Box and the Engine Shed. By far the most challenging is the Station Building with its intricate decorative stonework in the style of nearby Burghley House. A fifth structure would be the Midland signal box, which was removed in 1957 when branch trains started running to Stamford Town station, and all signalling transferred to the former GNR box.

The ex-Great Northern Signal Box overhung the River Welland and was supported by cantilevered timbers. The model of this box was the first produced in the Prototype Models range of card construction kits.

The Station Building at Stamford is on Water Street and is now a private house. The ornate frontage of the station building is based on the style of nearby Burghley House, home of the Marquis of Exeter.

The goods shed at Stamford East looking west. The stone part of the building now forms part of the Welland Mews housing development.

The Stamford engine shed interior looking towards the station. The shed had been extended to accommodate three locomotives when the Wansford branch was open. P H WELLS

LOCOMOTIVES USED

The Stamford and Essendine branch is best known for being home to Ivatt Class C12 4-4-2T locomotives, which had been displaced from London suburban services by Gresley N2 0-6-2Ts when they were introduced in 1923. When diesel multiple units took over from the N2s they too migrated northwards and could be seen on station pilot duties at Peterborough North and Grantham. In later years as the C12s aged, they were supplemented by former Great Central N5 0-6-2Ts, ironically even older than the C12s.

For the Essendine service there were always two locomotives in steam (except Sundays when there was no service) and they were stabled overnight in the single road engine shed, returning to New England shed at Peterborough for servicing on

C12 4-4-2T No 67357 was also a regular on the Stamford & Essendine branch. Model by Tony Wright from a Wills kit – the chimney and dome vary between classes, details to be wary of when modelling these locomotives. TONY WRIGHT

Saturday night and returning ready for duty early on Monday morning. They always faced bunker first towards Stamford, one locomotive would operate the passenger service, the other would shunt transfer freight to and from the Midland goods yard at Stamford Town station and pick up from Priory Sidings. It would then make up a goods train for Essendine and travel there around lunchtime, shunt and pick up goods for Stamford and return in the late afternoon. Goods trains returning to Stamford always used the left-hand platform facing the buffers - the former Wansford branch platform. Engineering work on the line was carried out on Sundays, usually with a J6 0-6-0 in charge.

Two early 4mm scale wagons by Slaters Plastikard lettered for the local gas works at Stamford. They were recently returned after a display in Stamford Museum.

Modelling Stamford East

Although these suggestions for modelling Stamford East show ideas in N, OO and O gauges, there's no reason why – subject to space – they couldn't be adapted to any scale. The fourth plan imagines that Stamford received its main line route.

STAMFORD EAST (17ft x 4ft, N gauge)

Even in N gauge a scale model of Stamford East station requires a length of at least 15ft as shown here. The former Midland line from Leicester to Peterborough is a continuous circuit with 12 staging roads off-scene at the rear of the model, with a two-track stub end yard to provide storage for the trip working to Stamford Town station. The branches to Essendine and Wansford, as well as the line to Priory Sidings run to a branch staging yard also at the rear of the layout.

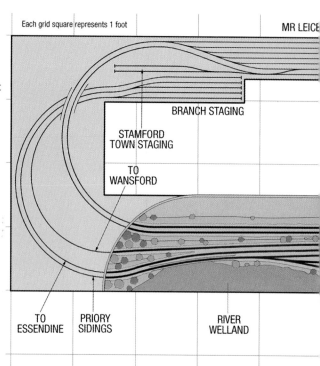

Each grid square represents 1 foot

MR LEICE[STER]

BRANCH STAGING

STAMFORD TOWN STAGING

TO WANSFORD

TO ESSENDINE

PRIORY SIDINGS

RIVER WELLAND

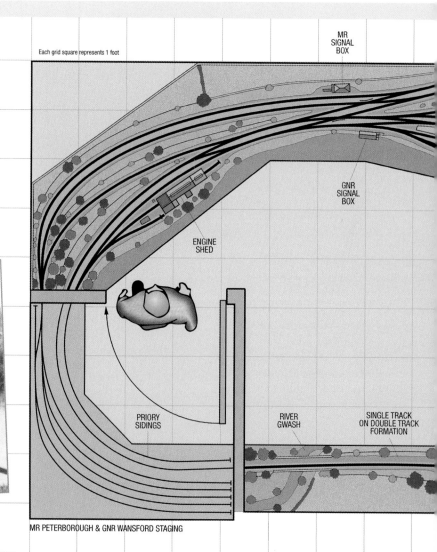

Each grid square represents 1 foot

MR SIGNAL BOX

GNR SIGNAL BOX

ENGINE SHED

PRIORY SIDINGS

RIVER GWASH

SINGLE TRACK ON DOUBLE TRACK FORMATION

MR PETERBOROUGH & GNR WANSFORD STAGING

This photograph shows the line's proximity to the River Welland. C12 4-4-2T No. 67392 is on the right on the line to Priory Sidings with the engine shed behind. Another C12 is off-scene to the left arriving with the branch passenger from Essendine.

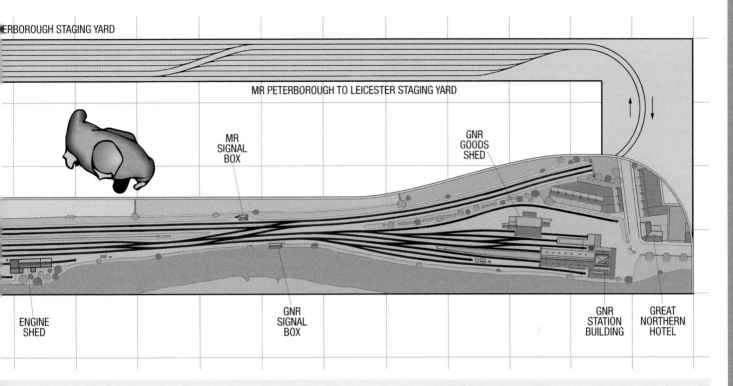

ERBOROUGH STAGING YARD

MR PETERBOROUGH TO LEICESTER STAGING YARD

MR SIGNAL BOX

GNR GOODS SHED

ENGINE SHED

GNR SIGNAL BOX

GNR STATION BUILDING

GREAT NORTHERN HOTEL

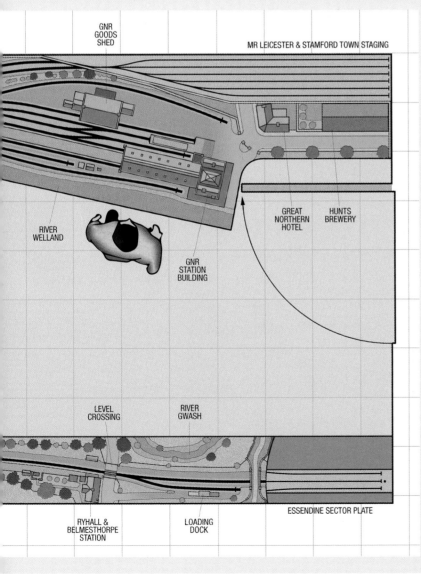

GNR GOODS SHED

MR LEICESTER & STAMFORD TOWN STAGING

RIVER WELLAND

GNR STATION BUILDING

GREAT NORTHERN HOTEL

HUNTS BREWERY

LEVEL CROSSING

RIVER GWASH

ESSENDINE SECTOR PLATE

RYHALL & BELMESTHORPE STATION

LOADING DOCK

STAMFORD EAST
(17ft 6ins x 9ft 6ins, OO gauge)

I had a garage which I'd converted into a railway room by replacing the up and over garage door with a stylish glazed frontage with a wider than usual door - handy for getting layouts in and out. My central heating boiler was in one corner, partitioned from the rest of the room. I drew the accompanying plan to see what features of Stamford East I could fit in the space and with some selective compression of the station managed to incorporate the intermediate branch station - Ryhall & Belmesthorpe - with a sector plate to represent the main line connection at Essendine. The Leicester to Peterborough line runs between stub end staging yards, the Leicester (and Stamford Town) tracks are behind the East Station backscene and the Peterborough (and Priory Sidings) tracks are in the boiler room.

A sleepy view of Ryhall and Belmesthorpe station - or 'Belmisthorpe' according to the platform sign - looking towards Essendine. Note the double track width of the right of way. R C RILEY

ESSENDINE IN A LARGE SHED (32ft x 12ft, OO gauge)

It's to the Stamford & Essendine's main line connection that I turn to for my largest plan. When my friend Tony Wright wanted a sizeable layout to do justice to his fleet of hand-built LNER 'Pacifics', our first thought was to model Essendine (which would also have given me somewhere to run my C12 tank locomotives). When I was gathering information for my college thesis BR were kind enough to supply me with the plan of Essendine as well as Stamford East, so I scaled the plans up to 4mm scale and drew the layout here to fit in Tony's railway shed - which measures 32ft x 12ft. You can see the BR plan underneath the drawn plan, and it shows where compromises had to be made at both ends to curve the layout round within the available space. As well as the branch coming in from Stamford, there was also a branch from Bourne until its closure in 1951, and trains on this branch had a variety of motive power from K2 2-6-0s to

Ivatt 4MT 2-6-0s, passengers being carried in a twin set composed of former GNR railmotor carriages. After much deliberation, it was decided to go for a simpler station and so the now well-known model of Little Bytham was opted for.

Essendine station looking north, with a C12 4-4-2T ready to leave for Stamford. There was a small yard to the left where goods from (and to) Stamford could be marshalled.

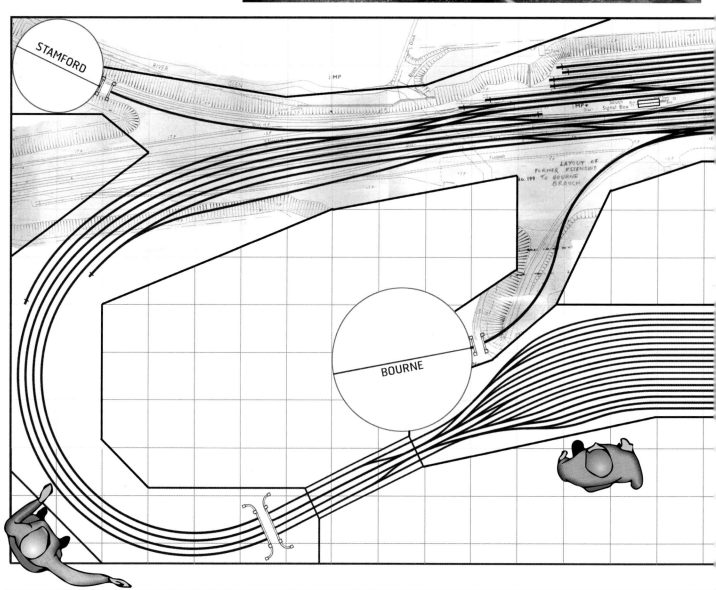

WHAT IF… GNR MAIN LINE THROUGH STAMFORD
(15ft x 8ft, OO gauge)

This prospect has always been in my mind, as countless 'might have been' plans in my files prove. The line would have struggled to find a way through the centre of the historic stone town and would probably have crossed the Welland to the east of the town before heading north to Grantham. It could still have had the branch to Wansford and a junction with the Midland route from Leicester to Peterborough, but in addition could have had a branch to Bourne (and a direct route on to Sleaford) with Essendine merely an intermediate station.

This plan provides the opportunity to mix main line running with branch line trains, with added operational interest created by the gasworks alongside the River Welland.

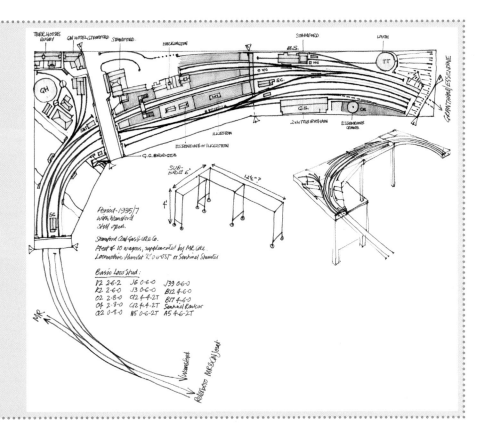

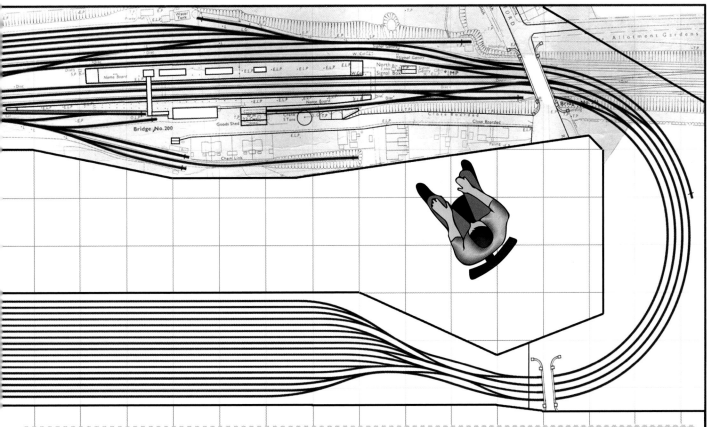

STAMFORD STATION: INTERESTING FACTS

■ It's often said that the 2nd Marquis of Exeter built the Stamford and Essendine at his expense and that the train guards wore his livery. While not strictly correct, the coat of arms is displayed on the facade of Stamford East station.

■ A memorable event took place in July 1878 when GNR 0-4-2ST No. 503 became derailed near the engine shed, rolled into the River Welland and was stuck there for over a week.

HORNBY®

R8217
Hornby Track Mat
£16.99

R8227 - TrackMat Accessories Pack 1
£36.99

R171
Single Home Signal
£10.99

R8221 – Track Extension Pack A
£16.99

R8222 – Track Extension Pack B
£29.99

R8228 - TrackMat Accessories Pack 2
£44.99

R169 – Junction
Home Signal
£14.99

R8223 – Track Extension Pack C
£27.99

R8229 - TrackMat Accessories Pack 3
£27.99

R8230 - TrackMat Accessories Pack 4
£44.99

R8226 – Track Extension Pack F
£27.99

R8231 - TrackMat Accessories Pack 5
£36.99

R172
Single Distant Signal
£10.99

TO SEE THESE AND THE REST OF THE HORNBY

HORNBY HOBBIES

Visit **www.hornby.com** to locate our nearest

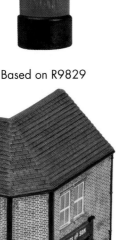

COTTLESTON

Inventing a town and railway was found to be the solution to run mixed motive power on this mid-noughties truncated branch line station.

Factfile

Layout name: Cottleston
Scale/gauge: OO gauge
Size: 12ft x 1ft 8in
Era/region: East Anglia 2007
Location: Fictitious
Layout type: Fiddleyard to station terminus
Owner: Ben Adlington
Photography: Paul Bason
See more: May 2009 **BRM**

After leaving the army Ben realised he could put schoolboy trainsets behind him and build a model railway. A few years and three abortive starts later, he realised inspiration and passion about the subject you choose to model is vital in seeing it through to completion. He learnt plenty from these builds, but claimed he spent too much time and money on whims that never progressed beyond track pinned to a baseboard. These half-built layouts would merely litter his garage.

Not a fan of steam locomotives or BR blue diesels and discovering he liked single-car DMUs, Ben settled on representing a modern branch line. He had hoped for a through station because he found branch line termini to be basic, but without room in his garage for an oval and two fiddleyards wouldn't fit length-ways.

A reverse station like Battersby, Bere Alston or Bourne End, with a fiddleyard at one end was a necessary compromise, but the other end suggests the line once continued elsewhere, with track now removed.

'Cottleston' is a fictional village with a fictional railway. Ben thought that in a different reality it would be in the north Nottinghamshire area, where lines of

Trackplan

MOGGS EYE
SIGNAL BOX

HOSIERY
FACTORY

0	1	2	3	4	5

0	0.5	1.0	1.5

competing railway companies once wove around each other as they fought over coal.

His original idea to 'crane shunt' stock failed and because a fan of sidings would take up too much space he built a rudimentary cassette system on a modified board, recovered from another project. ∎

> **Planning is key to a good model railway – it's rarely wasted and will save you time and money when you start building**"

FORMER
GOODS SHED

STATION
BUILDING

CROW LANE
SIGNAL BOX

2.0m

BACKDORE QUAY

The seagulls flying overhead are easily imagined on Dave Murdoch's London and South Western dock scene representing a 'could be' corner of Dorset.

Factfile

Layout name: Backdore Quay
Scale/gauge: O gauge
Size: 13ft 2in x 5ft (with proposed extension)
Era/region: L&SWR
Location: Fictitious
Layout type: Sector plate to sidings
Owner: Dave Murdoch
Photography: Tony Wright
See more: January 2005 **BRM**

Designed to free stand on top of kitchen units (less their tops) that run down one side of his workshop, Backdore Quay's plan was created as a shunting conundrum using the swing bridge as a sector plate. It was soon found that this was restrictive, one locomotive and six wagons being sufficient stock.

Dave's new plan intended to revise baseboard one (see trackplan) and make operation more in-keeping with railway practice. This would give scope for two people to play trains.

Screw and three-link couplings are used because traffic is light and uncoupling is described as laid back at best. Scenery is mainly made up of half-relief buildings to save space and because of these, Dave didn't feel the need to create a backscene as with his previous layout 'North Wareing'.

He found hand-building the track from C&L components to be difficult and thought copper clad sleepers to be of more use. ∎

Pros

I Locomotive shed at one end of the layout makes a good scenic change
I Swing bridge that doubles as a sector plate is a clever use of space

Cons

I Screw and three-link couplings are used because traffic is light
I Operation is laid back

"**Notwithstanding the absence of chairs, Dave feels more confident using copper clad construction for track, especially when making slips or three-way points using C&L components.**"

Trackplan

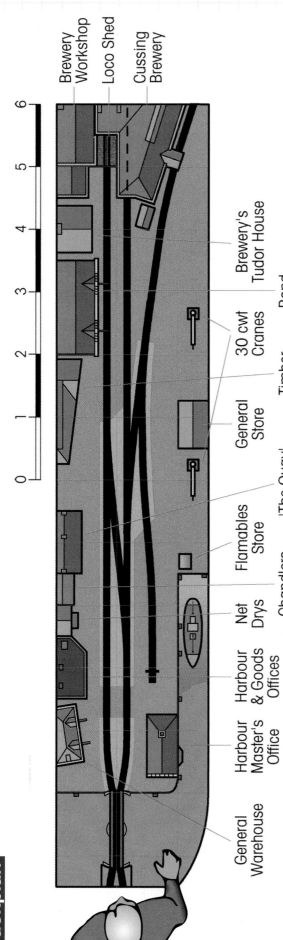

Brewery Workshop
Loco Shed
Cussing Brewery

6
5
4
3
2
1
0

Brewery's Tudor House

Bond

30 cwt Cranes

Timber Store

General Store

'The Quay' Hotel

Flamables Store

Chandlers

Net Drys

Harbour & Goods Offices

Harbour Master's Office

General Warehouse

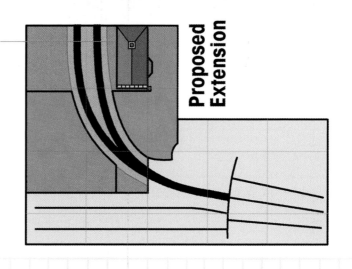

Proposed Extension

THISTLEMERE

Graeme Marriott and Colin Postlethwaite built this blue diesel era exhibition layout to experience more disciplines within the model-making hobby.

Having been involved with the construction of many exhibition layouts, mainly from a baseboard construction and electrics point of view, Graeme and Colin felt it was time to hone their skills at other aspects of the model-making hobby. The way to do this was to build their own layout from scratch.

The result was 'Thistlemere', a layout not based on anywhere in particular, but devised to give both modellers the experience of designing a layout and completing its scenic elements. The only constraint they had was that the layout had to be suitable for the rolling stock they owned - a 1970s/'80s period layout with blue/grey through to triple grey. That aside, anything was considered 'fair game'.

Track on all sections of the baseboards is Peco code 75 finescale. This was chosen as they wanted to get to the scenic stage of the layout build as early as possible. Points are operated with Seep point motors with integral switches, but they admit with hindsight, Tortoise or Fulgurex would be a better option. They've found a workaround is to use switch cleaner prior to an exhibition weekend.

Operation is via two control boxes mounted on large, flat-mount picture hooks. One controls stock via Gaugemaster hand-held controllers, points via a pen and

Trackplan

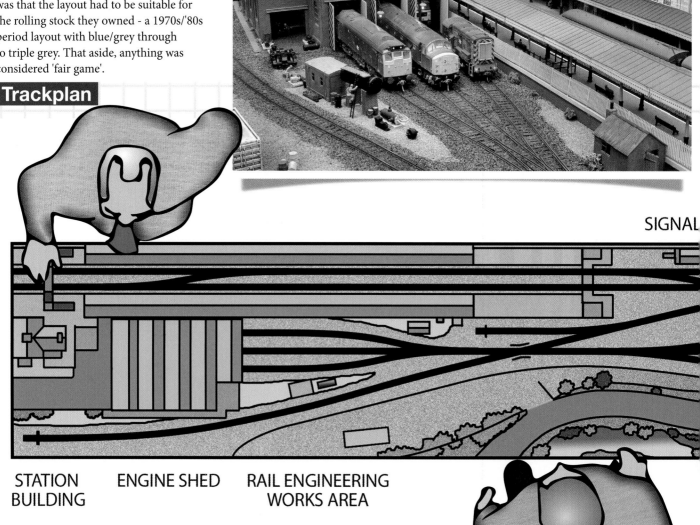

SIGNAL

STATION BUILDING   ENGINE SHED   RAIL ENGINEERING WORKS AREA

Factfile

Layout name: Thistlemere
Scale/gauge: OO gauge
Size: 13ft 6in x 2ft
Era/region: 1970s/1980s BR blue
Location: Ficticious
Layout type: Fiddleyard to storage roads
Owner: Graeme Marriott and Colin Postlethwaite
See more: May 2007 **BRM**

Pros

I Use of proprietry track speeds up this stage of the build - useful if you'd rather build scenery sooner if you enjoy that more
I Three areas of interest to entertain

Cons

I Seep point motors proved unreliable because of the integral switch
I Think about track cleaning when planning - inside depots, under canopies and bridges

studs on the panel, and section control via switches configured for cab control.

The fiddleyard at the rear of the goods yard board has three tracks for the line approaching the station and one for the other. The extension board is used to enable four-coach trains to be operated at exhibitions and to act as storage for stock. Shunting of stock and running round in the station is assisted by magnets recessed into the board bases. Placement of these was critical, especially on the reception siding as it has a slight curve.

The layout can be divided into three main areas of interest - the station allowing trains to stop and depart, the engine shed offering possibilities for moving locomotives on and off shed - even leaving them 'on show' for viewers to admire - and the freight depot which can be shunted at will. The overbridge divides the layout into two halves whilst hiding access to the fiddleyard. ∎

> " The buildings were either kit or scratch-built allowing Graeme and Colin to develop their construction skills "

0   1   2   3   4   5   6

STORAGE ROADS

SHOPS   WEIGHBRIDGE   DIESEL FUEL   FREIGHT DEPOT

SALMON PASTURES

LMS meets LNER meets BR on this depot layout which draws its creativity from childhood memories spent in the Sheffield area by its builder.

Factfile

Layout name: Salmon Pastures
Scale/gauge: OO gauge
Size: 12ft x 6ft
Era/region: 1930s-1950s LNER/LMS and BR
Location: Sheffield
Layout type: Fiddle yards to locomotive sheds
Owner: S. Burdett
Photography: Ray Lightfoot
See more: May 2009 **BRM**

Measuring 12ft in length, 'Salmon Pastures' offers a lot of activity for its space. Divided into two sections, with a scenic section that extends around its left-hand side, it's first area of operation lies with its town scene and foundry. It's here at its left side that you'll find two sidings separate from the rest of the layout. Adding height to the layout, a retaining wall supports a street scene to the rear featuring a corner pub, and industrial buildings, whilst a passing tram runs the full length of the layout, disappearing off-scene behind a building.

The main section of the layout also makes use of two different heights, access to which can be from one of two fiddle yards to the rear where lines disappear off-scene through tunnels.

The main purpose of this layout was to display locomotives and recall youthful memories of 'bunking' around sheds, so it's hardly surprising that an LNER shed scene dominates so much of the layout. Keeping it interesting – but plausible – was a requirement, so features such as the turntable and raised coaling stage justify movements around the shed, whilst two locomotive sheds set in the LMS and LNER styles mingle with a water tower and sand drier.

'Salmon Pastures' sizeable fiddle yard copes admirably with the length of trains that circulate because no lengthy express or freight trains are required. ■

> **The turntable and raised coaling stage justify movements around the shed, whilst two locomotive sheds set in the LMS and LNER styles mingle**

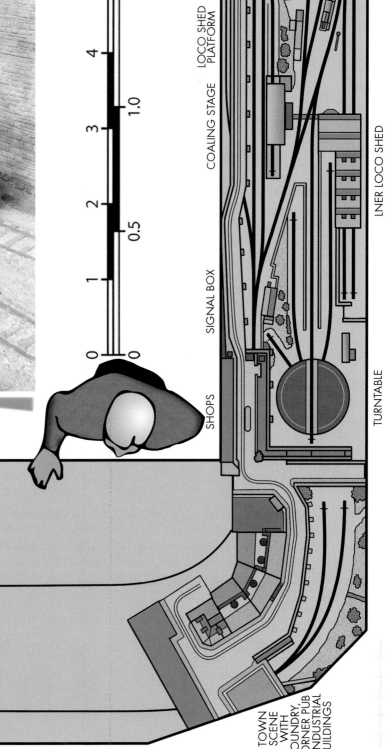

WATER TOWER

SAND DRYER

LMS LOCO SHED

LOCO SHED PLATFORM

COALING STAGE

LNER LOCO SHED

SIGNAL BOX

TURNTABLE

SHOPS

TOWN SCENE WITH FOUNDRY, CORNER PUB & INDUSTRIAL BUILDINGS

6ft

2.0m

5 — 1.5

4 — 1.0

3

2 — 0.5

1

0 — 0

Pros

I Working turntable
I Two sheds each house different stables of motive power
I Retaining walls with buildings form a more natural backdrop than a painted backscene

Cons

I Three fiddleyards need careful management to avoid forgetful mistakes

Trackplan

ALSTON

A confirmed fan of BR steam in the north east of England, choosing a scale and a subject to model proved a little harder for Dave Smith.

Factfile

Layout name: Alston
Scale/gauge: N gauge
Size: 10ft x 7ft
Era/region: BR 1950s
Location: North East
Layout type: Sector plate to terminus
Owner: Dave Smith
Photography: Tony Wright
See more: April 2006 **BRM**

Back in 1994, after a barren modelling period Dave bthought it was right to start again. Living some 200 miles from his home club and having experienced the frustration of taking on too big a garden railway project, he wanted his next project to be manageable in the limited time and space he had available.

Some decisions were easy like choosing its location which would be the North East of England in BR steam days. What to model, what scale and what standards he found were more difficult questions. He always felt that model railways should be just that, a railway not just a collection of stock, however good, squeezed into an unrealistic space. The space he had available was an approximately 10ft square room, which pointed him towards N gauge, a scale he'd never worked in before, so research was needed. This established that whilst there was limitation regarding stock, there could be enough available to make a start.

At this point he took a step forward and joined the N Gauge Society, perused its information and visited as many exhibitions as he could to view layouts and suppliers.

He still hadn't decided on a specific location, more research of magazines and books followed, but it was when an article appeared in *British Railways Illustrated* depicting Alston, also featured in Ken Hoole's *North-Eastern Branch Line Temini* that he was sold on the location. These two publications together with Stanley Jenkins history of the branch gave him enough photographs and drawings of the interesting location to make a start with his son Philip on some of the station buildings.

With the buildings completed, they decided to make a start building the rest of the layout. Many sessions on a photocopier produced a 2mm scale drawing of the 1923 version of the station layout. This was fixed to the baseboards and Dave discovered that by some miracle he found that the station area from the Hexham road at the rear to the front siding and the end wall by the turntable pit to the signal box fitted neatly onto the first 4ft x 2ft board.

Only a small amount of juggling was needed to avoid a point over the baseboard joint. The crossover and Down sidings were then fitted into the rest of the front section of the layout and were curved round the

'L' to the first bridge over the railway. This bridge disguises the entrance to the fiddle yard, which consists of a six-track sector plate with its own inbuilt sector plate at the end to release locomotives. ∎

Pros

I Fiddle yard accessible from branch and Down sidings head shunt
I Portrays a railway in a landscape
I Point templates used when laying track

Cons

I Pilot locomotive required - no passing loop in station
I Two person operation required to expolit the trackplan to its fullest

With the buildings completed, they started building the rest of the layout. Many sessions on a photocopier produced a 2mm scale drawing of the 1923 station layout"

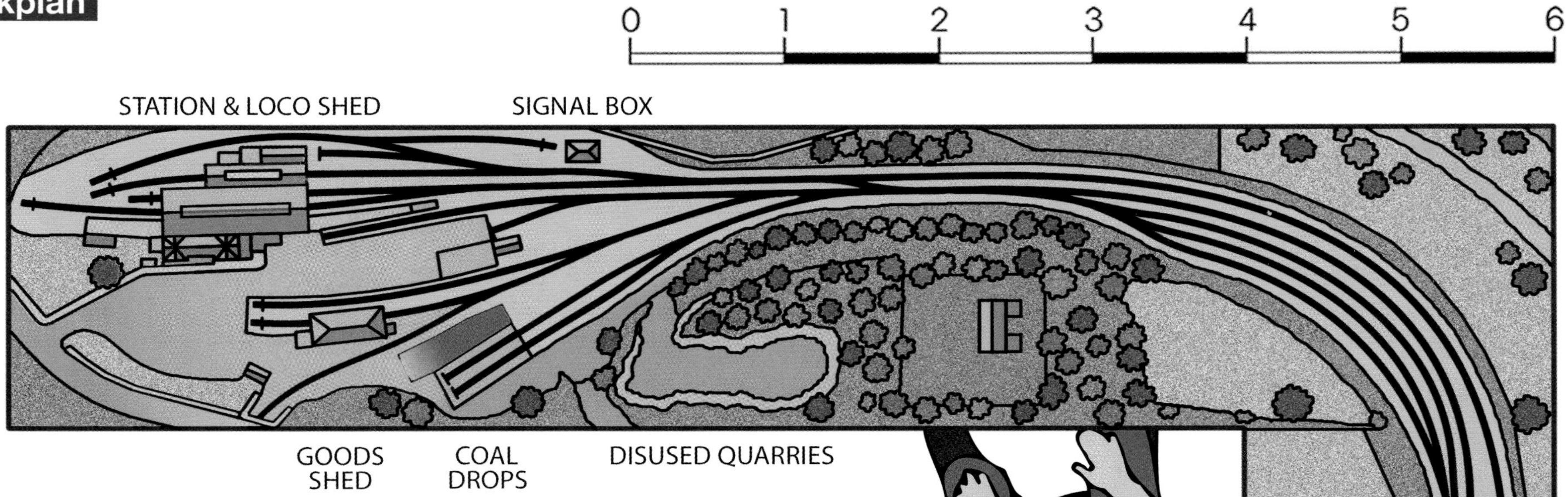

6

5

4

3

2

1

0

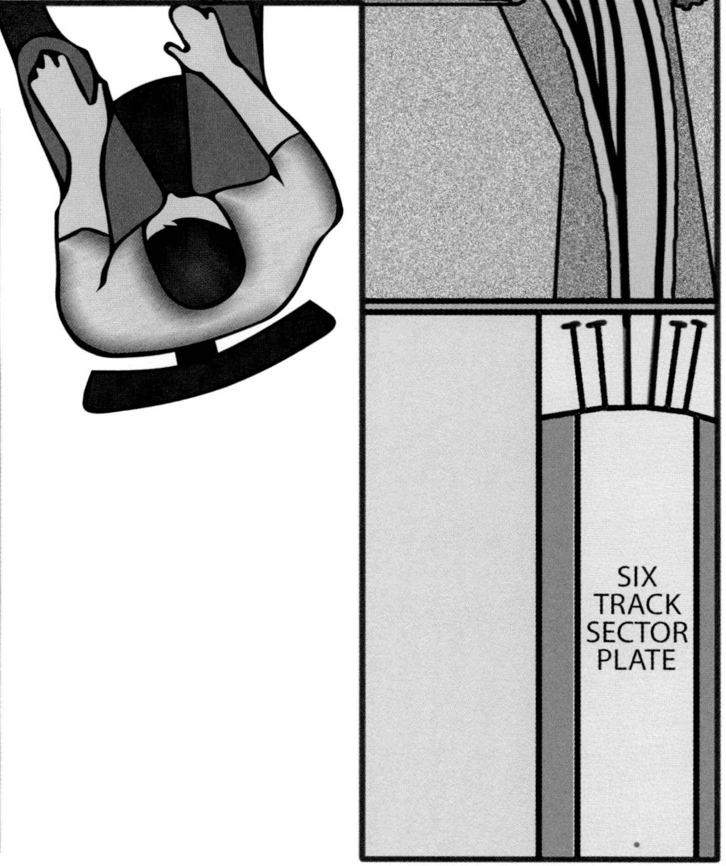

SIX TRACK SECTOR PLATE

STATION & LOCO SHED

SIGNAL BOX

GOODS SHED

COAL DROPS

DISUSED QUARRIES

TALYLLYN ROAD

Andy Cundick's Brecon & Merthyr/Cambrian layout evolved from an EM gauge test track and employs a clever space-saving sector plate.

In his own words, an accumulation of EM gauge stock over the years reached the point where they needed something to be run on. 'Etterick' a design in Ian Rice's book Light Railway Designs caught Andy's eye. It had what he was looking for, namely room to operate both mainline and industrial locomotives with opportunities for shunting.

The only significant change he made was to move the location from the Scottish Borders to the Welsh Marches, because this area saw the meeting of companies such as the GW, LNW, Midlands, Cambrian, Brecon & Meythr and Neath & Brecon. The date chosen for his model was 1920.

The baseboards were constructed from 0.5in marine ply, with a frame made from 2in x 1in timber. Built to a length of 4ft, the boards comfortably fit into the back of his Land Rovers.

Track used throughout is a mixture of SMP and Ratio track bases with the points

being made from copper clad (PCB) strip, operated using slider switches to change points and their polarities. The electrics are kept simple with a Gaugemaster 12V DC hand-held feedback controller providing

power. The only signal is operated by a solenoid, whilst uncouplers powered by electro-magnets are positioned in sidings where necessary, making exhibition performances smooth. ∎

Trackplan

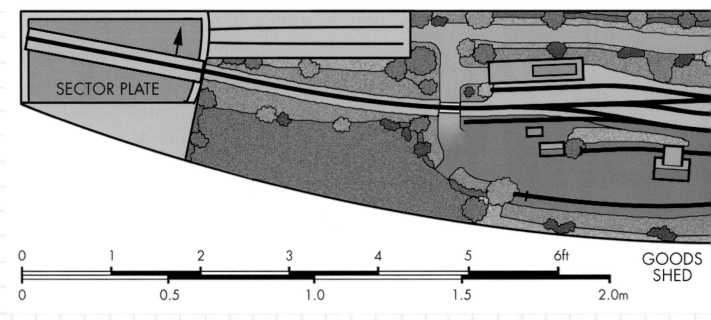

CATTLE DOCK

SECTOR PLATE

GOODS SHED

0   1   2   3   4   5   6ft

0   0.5   1.0   1.5   2.0m

Factfile

Layout name: Talyllyn Road
Scale/gauge: EM gauge
Size: 16ft x 2ft 6in
Era/region: Brecon & Merthyr/Cambrian 1920
Location: Fictitious
Layout type: Sector plate to traverser
Owner: Andy Cundick
Photography: Ray Lightfoot
See more: December 2009 **BRM**

Pros

I Flowing design with passing loops to permit shunting of traffic between trains
I Raised banks create the illusion of a railway in a cutting
I Kick-back sector plate allows more scenery for the same space

Cons

I Curved layout front makes the design more interesting, but adds little

> "'Etterick' a design in Ian Rice's book Light Railway Designs caught Andy's eye."

TATION BUILDING

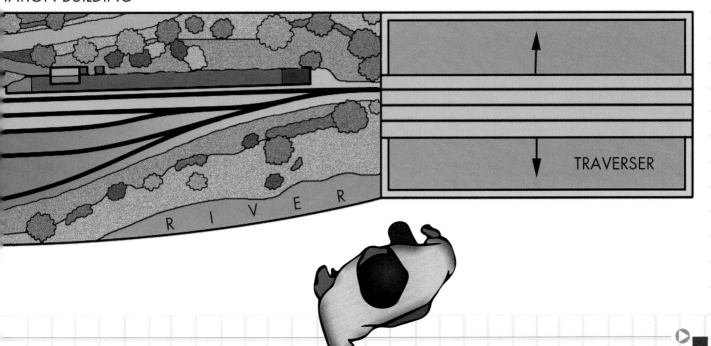

RIVER

TRAVERSER

TAPLEY

Colin Chisem's creation depicts a timeless typically English GWR branch line scene, with ideas drawn from a real location.

Colin has always felt that model railways should be atmospheric things and that they should bring to mind a specific period in the history of our country. It was this that motivated him to produce a model of a quiet country railway, with a pretty simple trackplan and plenty of scenery - 'Tapley' was the result.

The inspiration for 'Tapley' came from a careful consideration of the small stations on the Abbotsbury branch and particularly the station at Portesham. Colin was impressed with the simplicity of the station at Portesham and he set about trying to produce something which would resemble the scene. With photographs to work from models of the buildings could be produced. The original plan on which he embarked was to build a model of Portesham station and the first two years of the project were

devoted to this end. However, having realised that the production of a scale model of an actual location wasn't as easy as he first thought, and that the atmosphere he was looking for was poroving to be elusive, he began to think about adding an additional siding to create more interest visually and operationally.

The layout including fiddleyards at each end measures 23ft 6in x 2ft 8in. His

model is that of a through station, with a goods/passing loop, a dedicated goods siding served by a goods shed and crane, a headshunt and a lay-by siding.

The layout is intended to represent a GWR branch line somewhere in the Cotswold countryside. The station and its yard are surrounded by hills and fields, suitably adorned with trees, hedges and bushes in an attempt to capture a peaceful country effect. Larger Elm trees feature at the front of the layout for more interest.

Pros ✓

I A convincing GWR branchline scene - a favourite subject for model railway builders
I This was the builder's third layout who had gained experience - getting the scenery right forms a big part of a scene like this

Cons ✗

I Countryside branchlines mustn't be treated the same way as a busy mainline - restraint on what to include and what to omit is required.

Factfile

Layout name: Tapley
Scale/gauge: OO gauge
Size: 11ft 6in x 2ft 8in
Era/region: 1936 GWR
Location: Loosely based on Abbotsbury branch
Layout type: Fiddleyard to fiddleyard
Owner: Colin Chisem
See more: August 2007 **BRM**

Trackplan

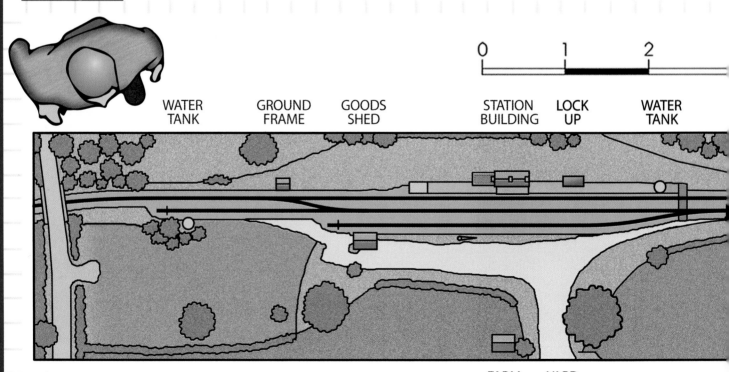

WATER TANK   GROUND FRAME   GOODS SHED   STATION BUILDING   LOCK UP   WATER TANK

FARM HUT   YARD GATE

0   1   2

On most model railways an element of compromise is involved, usually to compress lengths of passing loops and sidings. Colin discovered that the loop at Tapley matches that which existed at Portesham in length, accepting 15 goods wagons - a luxury he hasn't been able to afford in his previous attempts at railway modelling. He feels the results give a pleasing prototype look to the station yard when viewed from both ends of the layout.

All baseboards were built by a friend of Colin, meaning that all he had to do to get started was lay track. Buying pre-made baseboards is an option considered and used by many layout builders. Pre-made 'off the shelf' or 'made to order' baseboards offer a precise, neat and hassle-free way to getting your model railway off to a flying start.

Over the boards, Peco code 100 track was laid using large radius electrofrog points. 'Tapley' has a simple trackplan, so there are five buildings on the model. The station building and goods shed are based on those at Portesham on the Abbotsbury branch.

Colin enjoys layout operation as much as building layouts and he feels that although 'Tapley' has a simple station, a surprising number of train movements can be acheived. Trains can be seen waiting in the station for the 'Down goods' to drift into the loop, prior to shunting. Shunting movements can be performed from both ends of the station. ■

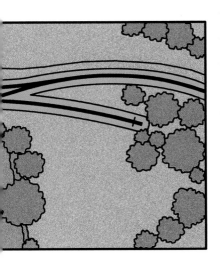

LOFTUS ROAD

Worthing MRC built this up-to-date model of a busy West London station.

At the beginning of 2005, other projects within Worthing MRC were nearing completion, so Pete Hollman put forward a project proposal for committee approval using modular baseboards that had been designed and built for a previous project that remained uncompleted.

The model was to be based around the West London line - a location which lends itself to a variety of traffic types as the line is a key link between the north and west of the country with the south and continent via the channel tunnel.

'Loftus Road' is a through station situated somewhere between Willesden and Clapham Junction and is very loosely based on Kensington Olympia. The time line is late 1990s through to the present day which offers a greater choice in train movements. On the passenger side are local surburban services, north/south cross country services

and empty Eurostar services, whilst on the freight side, Freightliner services, aggregates, various 'Channel Tunnel'-bound services and even the occasional nuclear flask. Add to this the various infrastructure trains and light engine movements and the operational scope is very wide.

The layout is a continuous-run oval, with the scenic part of the layout measuring 12ft, connecting to a 12ft modular fiddle yard which can also be used for other club projects.

Electrically, the layout is controlled by DCC with lights and sound fitted on many

of the locomotives and EMUs, but such is the flexibility of its construction it can also be operated in traditional DC mode should it be so desired.

As 'Loftus Road' was the first project to be slotted in to modular baseboards by the club, the fiddle yard needed to be built first. It took the best part of two years to get the track down, install the track, wiring and designing control panels for DCC or analogue use.

Control is kept as straightforward as possible with route selection via a single push button switch, a matrix diode and

> " **Loftus Road is a through station situated somewhere between Willesden and Clapham Junction** "

Trackplan

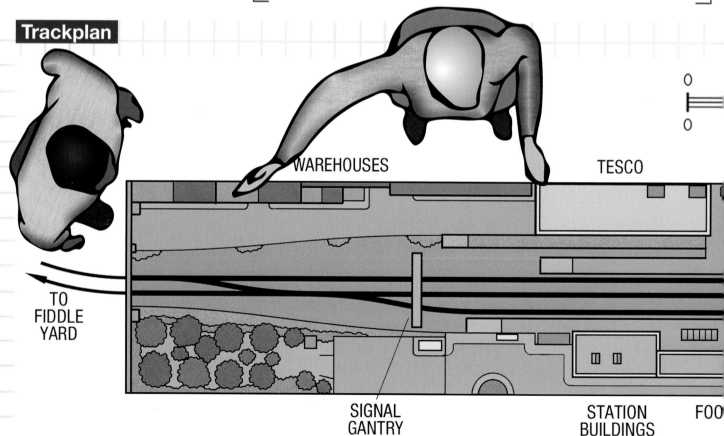

TO FIDDLE YARD

WAREHOUSES

TESCO

SIGNAL GANTRY

STATION BUILDINGS

FOO

Track used throught the layout is Peco code 75 'Streamline', with the third rail constructed with insulators and code 60 rail also from Peco, laid on a cork base ballasted with N gauge granite chippings and weathered.

Initially, the front boards were wired to enable either analogue running via cab control or digital control, but after a year or so it became apparent that the complex control panel on the front boards could lead to operating issues. The group was running exclusively DCC enabled stock, so they decided to remove all the section switches used for DC control and rewire the track, supplying the power via a two-wire bus and simplifying the point control from push buttons and relays to two-way toggle switches. This turned out to be an astute move, removing 'human error'. ∎

capacity discharge units. Switching between analogue and DCC control is via a single, four-pole toggle switch. To aid analogue users, each of the 12 fiddle yard roads is divided into two sections, with isolating switches. Power to the front boards is carried via the track and there is an Xpressnet feed for additional DCC controller ports for the Lenz set 100 system.

During the planning stage it was decided that Tortoise slow motion point motors would be used so the baseboard would need to be of sufficient depth to accommodate them. The three front boards measure 4ft x 2ft with a surface of 9mm MDF sheet, braced by 3in x 1in softwood and joined by 6mm bolts and aligned by brass dowles.

Factfile

Layout name: Loftus Road
Scale/gauge: OO gauge
Size: 12ft x 2ft
Era/region: 2000-present
Location: Fictitious (West London)
Layout type: Continuous loop
Owner: Worthing MRC
Photography: Richard Wilson
See more: June 2012 **BRM**

Pros ✓

I Combination of main line and rarely-modelled underground traffic
I Club members' specialities used well
I High-rise buildings create city atmosphere

Cons ✗

I Symmetrical trackplan is largely straight and parallel with layout front
I Kit-bashed buildings are key to setting the scene - many are required for this layout

1	2	3	4	5	6ft
0.5		1.0		1.5	2.0m

APARTMENTS   OFFICE BUILDINGS

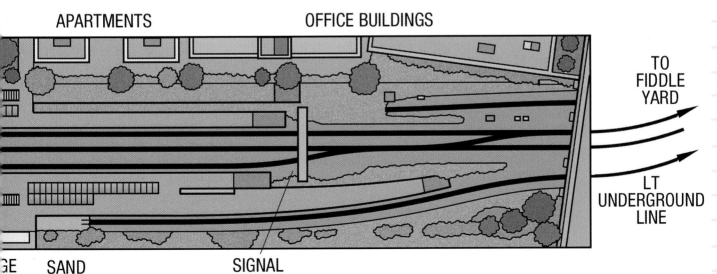

TO FIDDLE YARD

LT UNDERGROUND LINE

GE   SAND DRAG   SIGNAL GANTRY

BEECHES TMD

This DCC-operated modern diesel depot set in the north west was Paul Warburton's first OO gauge exhibition layout.

A t the age of 40, Paul's interest in model railways was rekindled. His N gauge layout in the garage was a steep learning and he soon realised that a garage or loft unless properly prepared is far from ideal with low temperatures in the winter to high temperatures in the summer.

This layout was sold and he began his transition into OO gauge. He prefers the scale over N gauge because his eyesight isn't what it once was and he finds it easier to work with.

Paul was interested in the line running along the north Wales coast and the last few decades has seen a huge diversity of locomotives and rolling stock with the added benefit of dramatic scenery and interesting locations such as the quarries and yard at Penmaenmawr and the aluminium works on Anglesey that closed in 2007.

Trackplan

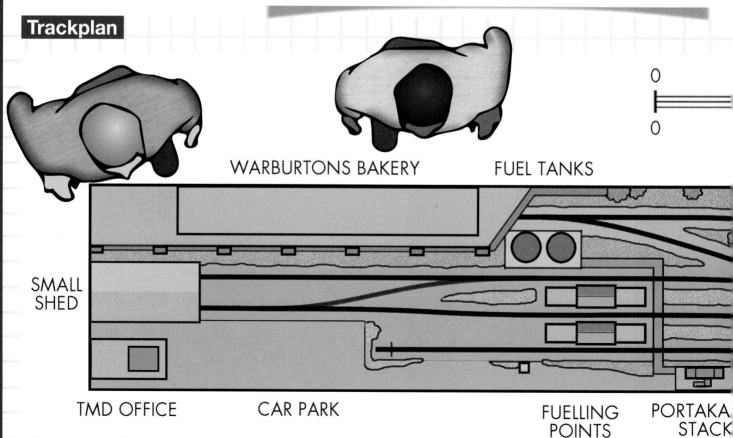

WARBURTONS BAKERY   FUEL TANKS

0

0

SMALL SHED

TMD OFFICE   CAR PARK   FUELLING POINTS   PORTAKA STACK

Factfile

Layout name: Beeches TMD
Scale/gauge: OO gauge
Size: 350cm x 50cm
Era/region: 1990s-2000s
Location: Fictitious (North West)
Layout type: Depot (sheds to sheds)
Owner: Paul Warburton
See more: April 2010 **BRM**

Pros

I Changing off-the-shelf models adds originality
I Buildings and vegetation add depth to the backscene

Cons

I Boards built on Sundeala warped
I Lack of fiddle yard at home reduces space required, but juggling stock is necessary and limits what can be displayed

Beeches TMD began early in 2007. Long-term, Paul hopes to have room for a larger layout, as he gets acquires more space, but in the meantime constraints meant a smaller end-to-end layout was his only option.

The location for the layout is fictitious, but set somewhere in the north west on the fringe of an urban area, with the foothills of north Wales in the background.

The left-hand end of the layout has two levels. On the lower level is a TMD office and car park and a two lane shed from the Pikestuff range. The office was made from Daler board as used by artists, with internal walls so that lighting could be added at a later date. It was hand-painted with acrylics and details like windows, doors, drainpipes and the TMD sign added. The upper

level covers a tunnel which was originally intended to disguise a small fiddle yard where he could conceal locomotives, whilst others were on the layout. An additional fiddle yard board was added for the layout's first exhibition.

Paul's hand-painted backscene obtained flattering comments at shows and reflects his interest in painting. Copper and green beech trees feature that lend their name to the layout. ∎

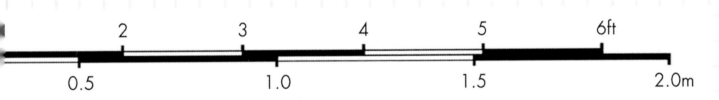

LOW RELIEF BACKSCENE

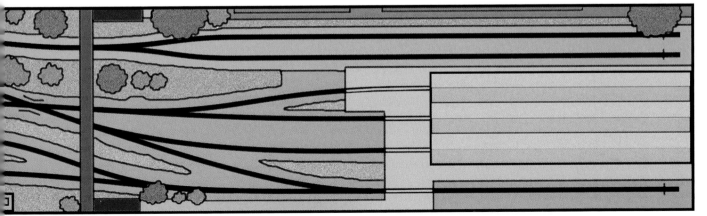

FOOTBRIDGE   MAIN MAINTENANCE SHED

FREE

WHEN YOU
SUBSCRIBE TO

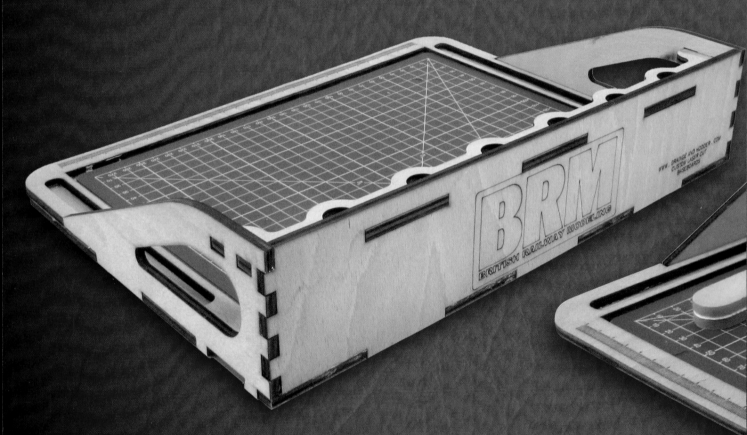

ABERDARE

This pre-grouping layout from the Cardiff 4mm group is a snapshot of the Taff Vale Railway and its 'black gold' from the Welsh coalfields.

Factfile

Layout name: Aberdare
Scale/gauge: OO gauge
Size: 11ft 6in x 8ft 2in
Era/region: Taff Vale Railway 1922
Location: South Wales
Layout type: Continuous loop
Owner: Cardiff 4mm group
Photography: Tony Wright
See more: January 2009 **BRM**

Of all the layouts built by the Cardiff 4mm group, they all agree that 'Aberdare' is the most interesting to operate. Its variety in part comes from the fact that the station is both a terminus and a through station, it has engine sheds, there are opportunities for shunting and the layout is relatively complex for its size.

After a decade of construction, the layout was finally completed in 1996. 'Aberdare' was built to fit in a group member's spare bedroom, but was later extended by 2ft to improve it visually whilst allowing longer trains to run.

The group finds that one of the attractions of modelling real locations is the complexity of simple details – in this instance the platforms which had been extended over many years with different brickwork. To create an accurate representation of subtle details, a few site visits were organised where photographs and measurements could be taken.

To create its north signal box, some good quality photographs were available, but for the others the group had to rely largely on aerial views.

The layout is wired with a common return using two controllers, one for Up and one for Down trains, although the wiring is arranged so that each controller can operate trains on any part of the layout. Points are operated by 'push-to-make' button switches. ∎

Pros

I Careful research of a location's history pays dividends when recreating the past
I Good use of Aerofilms archive aerial footage and OS maps
I Distances between points at layout fronts

Cons

I A decade to complete the layout – consider project management and timescales when working together, it's easy to get distracted
I Baseboards were built with chipboard tops and have sagged over the year

 After a decade of construction, 'Aberdare' was finally completed in 1996, built to fit in a group member's spare bedroom. It was later extended by 2ft to improve it visually

OO GAUGE

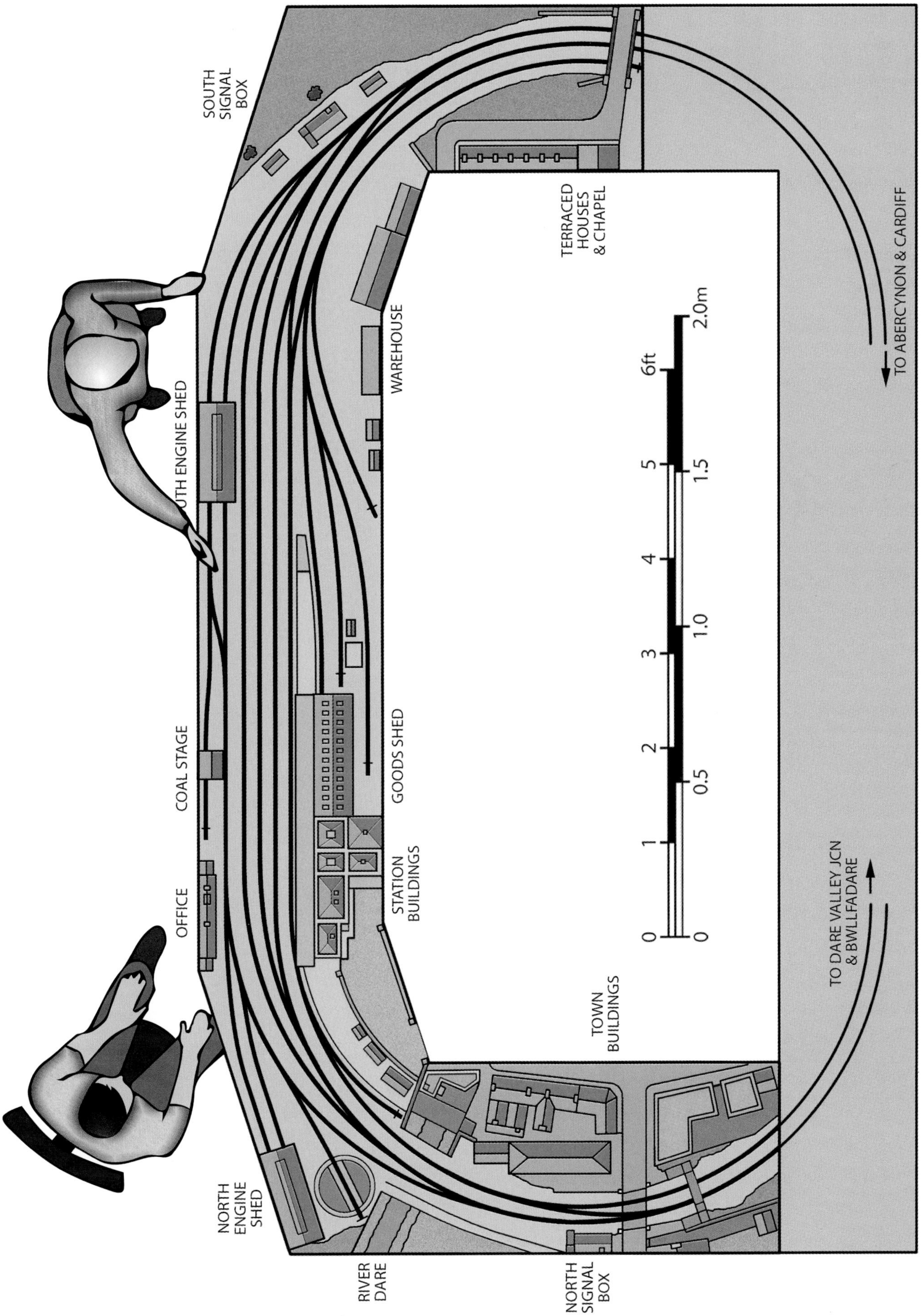

SOUTH SIGNAL BOX

SOUTH ENGINE SHED

COAL STAGE

OFFICE

NORTH ENGINE SHED

RIVER DARE

NORTH SIGNAL BOX

WAREHOUSE

GOODS SHED

STATION BUILDINGS

TERRACED HOUSES & CHAPEL

TOWN BUILDINGS

TO ABERCYNON & CARDIFF

TO DARE VALLEY JCN & BWLLFADARE

6ft

2.0m

0 1 2 3 4 5

0 0.5 1.0 1.5

GOLDHANGER

This essay in Essex light railway modelling by Roger Ford employs a simplistic trackplan which typifies the Kelvedon & Tollesbury Light Railway in the 1930s.

Trackplan

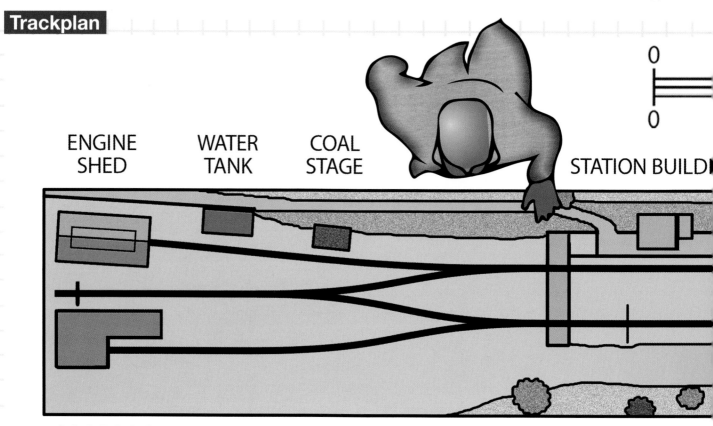

ENGINE SHED   WATER TANK   COAL STAGE   STATION BUILDI

GOODS DOCK

In 1995, due to a change of circumstances, Roger found himself living in a small flat with an 'L'-shaped bedroom. The unusual design meant there was a free wall, 12ft 6in long, which he thought was crying out to have a model railway built along it. At the time he was already thinking of moving up to O gauge, so could he build a layout in this space?

Roger wanted a layout that was prototypical, or that was at least based on prototype practice, so having always lived in Essex, his first thoughts turned to modelling one of the country's rural branch lines. Some initial research, looking at photographs and trackplans, showed that layouts, even compressed, wouldn't fit the space available.

He then came across some pictures of the Kelvedon & Tollesbury Light Railway. This was a somewhat eccentric line, which had an odd mixture of rolling stock, that ran from the former Great Eastern main line at Kelvedon through the middle of nowhere down to the Essex marshes and the river Blackwater. The line closed to passengers in 1951. However, an advantage of modelling a railway that has been closed for more than 40 years is that it's much harder for the 'rivet counters' to say you've got something wrong.

A second-hand copy of *The Tollesbury Branch* by Peter Paye was obtained, which provided photographs, descriptions and trackplans. The first thing of note was that track layouts were simple, so building pointwork and laying track would be quite straightforward. Secondly, being a light railway, the buildings on the line were few in number and of a very simple design, so would be appropriate for his limited abilities with plastic sheet modelling. Finally, only a limited amount of rolling stock ever operated on the line, and just about everything that was required was available in kit form. It seemed he'd found a layout that could be built in a reasonable space and amount of time.

Track layouts on the light railway were very basic, and most of the passing stations had simple track layouts as to offer almost no operating interest. Not being able to find a suitable location meeting his requirements, he settled upon a fictitious station.

The track plan is shown in the accompanying diagram. To see if the trackplan he proposed could be acheived, he drew a full-size trackplan and by using 'Y' points throughout, enough space could be saved to fit the platform, headshunts and sidings of adequate length. ∎

Factfile

Layout name: Goldhanger
Scale/gauge: O gauge
Size: 12ft 6in x 2ft
Era/region: K&TLR 1930s
Location: Fictitious (Kent)
Layout type: Fiddle yard to light railway station
Owner: Roger Ford
Photography: Ray Lightfoot
See more: December 2008 **BRM**

Pros

I Baseboards designed to avoid pointwork
I 'Y' points save valuavble space
I Four road traverser used 'off-scene'

Cons

I Only room to install traverser at an exhibiton, preventing full use at home
I Can be difficult to obtain information on more obscure

> " Roger wanted a layout that was based on prototype practice, so he modelled one of the country's rural branch lines "

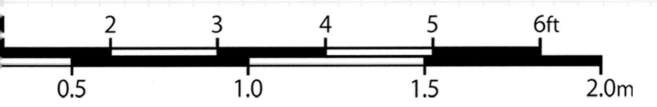

SIGNAL BOX

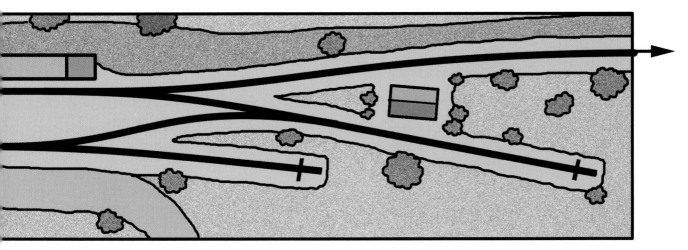

DALESIDE PARKWAY

Building a mainline layout to watch the passing of lengthy trains opened a door of opportunities for Brian Chawner and Fred Holt.

Rail traffic on the main line consists of inter-city expresses, DMU services and a selection of different freight traffic flows. The upper level of the layout is a four-track main line running through a principal 'Parkway' station with a local shuttle service operating to and from the bay platform. The lower level is a two-track mainline, electrified with overhead catenary allowing a fleet of electric locomotives to operate.

The layout is operated from its centre. Fiddleyards run the full length of the layout, connected to a further two 6ft 'jumper' fiddle road boards which connect to the main scenic sections of the layout. 'Daleside Parkway' requires four operators because the storage sidings can hold up to 50 scale length trains. Operator one controls the inner slow lines which run through platform one. Operator two controls the inner faster lines and outer lower main line. Operator

three controls the outer fast lines and inner lower main line, whilst operator four has the outer slow lines runn through platform two.

The shuttle service to the bay platform is operated automatically, controlling up to three trains for local services to and from 'Daleside'. The lower level main lines

run independently from those above and have their own storage sidings located at the rear of the scenic side of the layout. The fiddleyard exits are hidden in tunnels, avoiding the problem of unrealistic track curvature and the choice of what to place around the curves to fill awkward spaces. ∎

Trackplan

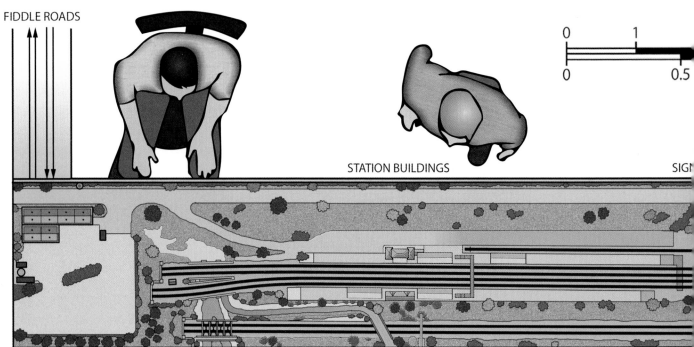

FIDDLE ROADS

STATION BUILDINGS

SIGN

0   1

0   0.5

TRANSPORT DEPOT   RIVER

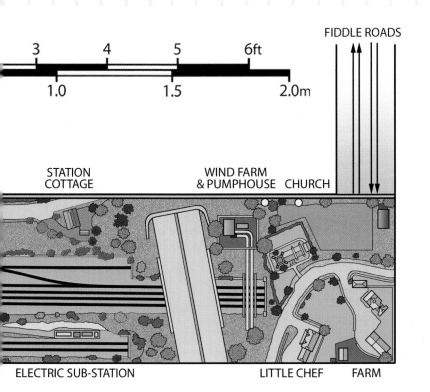

3　　　4　　　5　　　6ft

1.0　　　1.5　　　2.0m

FIDDLE ROADS

STATION
COTTAGE

WIND FARM
& PUMPHOUSE　CHURCH

ELECTRIC SUB-STATION

LITTLE CHEF　　FARM

Factfile

Layout name: Daleside Parkway
Scale/gauge: N gauge
Size: 16ft x 12ft
Era/region: Network Rail 1980s-present
Location: Fictitious
Layout type: Fiddleyard to fiddleyard
Owners: Brian Chawner and Fred Holt
Photography: Tony Wright
See more: February 2009 **BRM**

Pros

l Tunnels help conceal the excessive
and unrealistic track curvature to fiddleyards
l Ideal trackplan for intensive operations

Cons

l Manning a four-operator layout at
exhibitions is more expensive - automating
the lower level main lines would help
l Fiddle roads don't allow the rotation of
stock - not a problem with multiple units, but
something of a challenge with freight trains

CHEDDAR

Chris and Simon Challis' Somerset and Dorset Joint Railway theme
in P4 imagines the building of a proposed line to Cheddar.

The layout 'Cheddar' shows a S&DJR scene in the 1920s with stone, coal, general merchandise and passengers arriving and departing. The Cheddar Valley Oxide & Ochre mill was built after the line was opened.

The layout was constructed as an entry in the Scalefour Society 18.83 Layout Challenge - to build a layout to P4 standards in 18.83 square feet. The trackplan is taken from the Wild Swan book *Layouts for Small Spaces* by Iain Rice. Much use has been made of standard products; SMP phosphor bronze rail track, Ratio and Wills kits, Slater's Plastikard for the mill and Woodland Scenics for the grass and foliage.

The Somerset & Dorset Joint Railway never built the proposed line to Cheddar, but that doesn't mean prototype operation cannot be carried out. Being a terminus,

operation isn't just a case of running the trains through, or into the station stopping and carrying on - all trains terminate so have to be run-round or reformed before departure, creating small challenges.

Chris and Simon firmly believe that to operate prototypically you need a trackplan that follows prototype practice. For 'Cheddar' they found this easy because Iain Rice had worked out the trackplan using his knowledge. The thing is to know how the prototype worked, not so easy in

the case of 'Cheddar' which is set in a time period over 80 years ago. There are books on railway operation, but they don't give much detail. Ex-railwaymen have been consulted, each with their own different experiences; snippets have also been gleaned from books and magazines. A study of working timetables has also helped gain knowledge of how the prototype worked.

Being a light railway, there are no ground signals as all train and shunting movements within the station are carried out under the

> " Chris and Simon firmly believe that to operate prototypically you need a trackplan that follows prototype practice. "

Trackplan

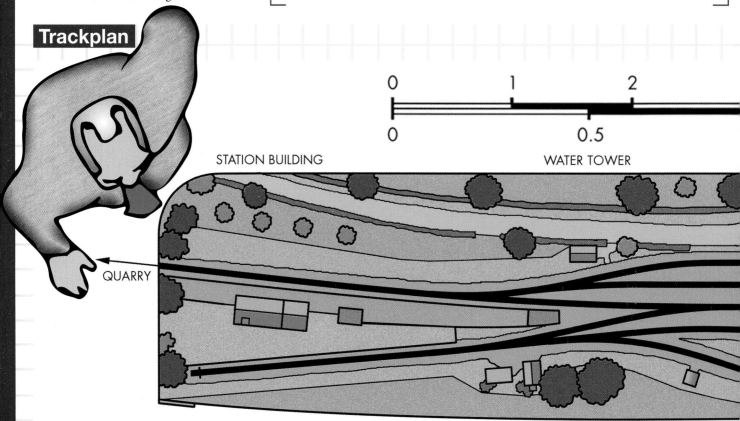

STATION BUILDING   WATER TOWER

0   1   2

0   0.5

QUARRY

HUTS

Factfile

Layout name: Cheddar
Scale/gauge: P4 gauge
Size: 8ft 6in x 2ft (plus fiddleyard)
Era/region: 1920s S&DJR
Location: Fictitious
Layout type: Fiddleyard to terminus
Owner: Chris and Simon Challis
Photography: Tony Wright
See more: January 2010 **BRM**

Pros

I Run-round loop away from station makes the marshalling of coaches more interesting
I Atmospheric area of the country to model

Cons

I P4 offers finer track standards, but all rolling stock must be converted - not just with new wheelsets, but compensation to avoid derailments

instruction of the shunter or the signalman giving flag signals from his signal box.

The train, normally a locomotive and two or three coaches, runs across the scene and into the platform, for 'would be' passengers to get out and parcels to be unloaded. You'll note from the trackplan that the run-round loop isn't by the platform. The locomotive has to propel the train back to the run-round loop where it uncouples, pulls forward, goes back through the run-round

loop and buffers up to the coach at the other end of the train.

A nice touch on uncoupling and coupling is to leave a little time for the screw coupling to be removed or applied and the brake and heating pipes to be disconnected or reconnected. At a small station like 'Cheddar' this was normally done by the fireman.

To make shunting wagons more interesting, some people either take

photographs of their wagons or record details on cards. Like a pack of playing cards they shuffle them and deal out the number of wagons that are required in a particular train. These wagons are then formed in the order the cards are dealt. When the train gets to a station the cards are combined with the cards of wagons in the sidings, shuffled again and dealt out. The train then has to be shunted into the new order, with wagons not dealt out left in the sidings. ∎

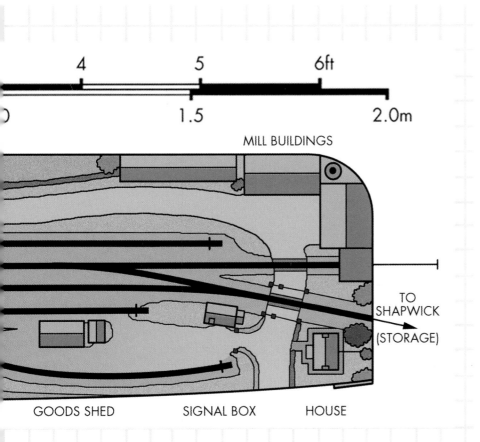

CULM

Jonathan Buckie's first attempt at EM gauge resulted in the creation of this GWR layout terminus with an attempt to deviate from the visual stereotype.

From the outset, Jonathan felt it was critical to consider how his layout would be presented. His preference is for layouts which are framed with a proscenium arch, a high backscene, side wings and a low lighting pelmet creating a 'letter-box' view which focuses the attention of viewers on the model and prevents eyes from wandering.

Two 4ft x 2ft baseboards were constructed from 6mm ply to an 'egg-box' design. These predate Culm having been built a year earlier for an aborted O-16.5 layout.

To detract from what would otherwise be a large 8ft box, a curved front section was added to the front edge which forms the river foundation and runs along the front of the model. The fiddle yard was constructed in the same way as the two main boards at 3ft in length.

A 15in backscene, integral to the layout, was constructed from 4mm flexi-ply and gently wraps around the rear of the scenic section to avoid corners appearing in the sky. A good quality, heavyweight lining paper was stuck to the ply to give a flat base on which to paint a simple, non-descript background.

To complete the 'framed' presentation a lighting pelmet was built from the same 6mm ply as used for the baseboards. Lighting is provided by two stripped-down 4ft warm-white florescent tubes which give an even 'soft' light.

The layout stands 3ft 6in high, supported on three trestles with ply 'T' beams slung between them. Jonathan feels the method of support makes setting up at exhibitions easier because the lightweight frame and be installed and levelled without needing to set the entire model up.

The trackplan is loosely based on Hemyock as it was prior to relaying in 1923, with features from other stations on the branch added where appropriate. The siding on the other side of the road hiding the entrance to the fiddle yard was borrowed from Uffculm. The cattle dock was taken from the post-1923 Hemyock trackplan with an end-load added.

In creating Culm, he didn't want to create 'another GWR branch line terminus', so there had to be something which would visually differentiate this layout from the stereotype. To achieve this, the platform was placed at the front between the viewer and the running line, forcing you to look around things and discover interesting cameos. Secondly, the Hemyock trackplan required all trains to set-back into the loop in order to run round, before being pushed back into

Trackplan

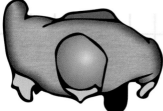

SIGNAL BOX   COAL STAITHES

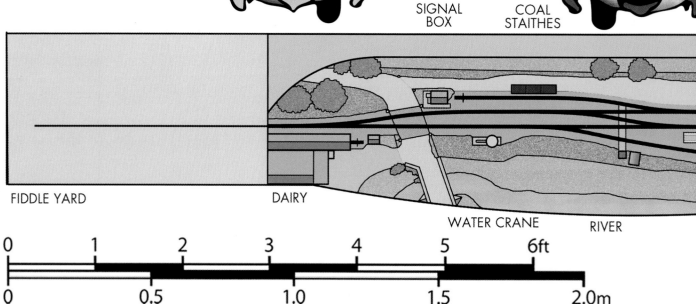

FIDDLE YARD   DAIRY

WATER CRANE   RIVER

| 0 | 1 | 2 | 3 | 4 | 5 | 6ft |

| 0 | 0.5 | 1.0 | 1.5 | 2.0m |

Factfile

Layout name: Culm
Scale/gauge: EM gauge
Size: 8ft x 2ft
Era/region: BR WR 1950s
Location: Fictitious
Layout type: Fiddleyard to terminus
Owner: Jonathan Buckie
Photography: Ray Lightfoot
See more: September 2009 **BRM**

Pros

I Track set away from layout front allows river to meander
I Dairy, accessible from fiddle yard removes need for an additional point

Cons

I One piece backscene at 8ft in length can be difficult to move around

the platform – this feature would ensure that action would take place along the whole length of the model rather than at one end.

Once a provisional trackplan was reached, lengths of flexi-track and EM gauge Society point templates were pinned to the cork top surface to see if it looked right, running through shunting moves to check for snags which could be easily cured rather than at a later date.

Track work is SMP and C&L flexi-track with Marcway points. Marcway points are an option when modelling to finer standards if you feel unable to construct your points. ■

YARD CRANE

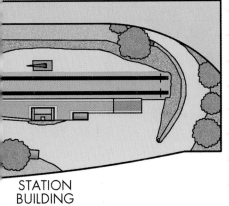

STATION BUILDING

PLANNING PENMAENMAWR

Looking for a viable subject to model to display a collection of kit-built ballast wagons, Howard Smith was drawn to this location on the north Wales coast.

On August 3, 1995, 31255 and 31188 double head the 6F11 to Warrington from Penmaenmawr sidings. The ZCV 'Plaice' wagons in the formation would only last a few more years in service. TONY BUCKTON

It was around 2003 that my foray into O gauge modelling began. Not being committed to a particular location, it was kits of locomotives and wagons that ran in the 1990s that I found interesting and hence built. Something drew me to the engineer's trains that were often made up of elderly vacuum-braked wagons that were due for replacement, yet somehow soldiered on in their often-tired liveries.

Location is key

It wasn't until I'd amassed a small collection of wagons that in 2009 I began to wonder where I'd run them. Looking around at photographs taken in the 1990s by my father, there was one location that instantly sold itself. A photograph taken of a Class 37 in Regional Railway livery on a mid-summers day in 1995 intrigued me. Here was a location adjacent to the Irish Sea, behind which the towering mountain - of the same name – offered a dramatic backdrop. Running parallel to the line was the A55 'express way' which weaved its way across via bridges where space wasn't available.

An aerial view of Penmaenmawr station, with the modelled area highlighted in red. Note the signalbox (left), subway adjacent, station building (centre) and ballast crushing plant (right). Below, the A55 was considered too large to model, so was omitted. Two long sidings allow wagons to be parked on the layout.

Penmaenmawr has been an important quarrying site for centuries – indeed, Tower Bridge in London is built from stone hewn from the site, but what interested me was the large stone crushing plant that took stone down the mountain via a series of conveyor belts, crushed it to the correct size for ballast, and loaded wagons in the sidings for distribution around the country.

Making a start

Research is key, but because I lived in France at the time, one of the easiest ways to start was the internet. Online help from RMweb (*www.RMweb.co.uk*) put me in contact with locals who had grown up in the area and could tell chapter and verse on how the location has changed over the years. Help from societies such as the London and North Western Railway Society (L&NWRS) gave me access to original plans of the footbridge, but nothing would give me every detail I needed – an onsite 'field trip' was required.

Field trip

Arriving at Penmaenmawr, I had a few essential details to measure. The signal box could be made without dimensions, counting the rows of bricks and transferring them to plastic brick sheet. This was a simple process and saved the need to approach network rail for site access which is off-platform. Armed with a few pens, a notepad and tape measure, I noted dimensions of the station building, station signage, bus shelter, and former goods shed. No field trip is complete without a camera and I made the most of the time there to record as many details as possible. A picture says a thousand words as the saying goes…

Aerial views

Google maps was in its infancy during the early stages of planning and didn't offer the 3-D views it does today, but it allowed me to plan what I'd model and what I'd leave out. Space wasn't a problem – the local club at Châtellerault had the underground basement of a large building at its disposal, so I could model the site to scale without compromise. Taking screen grabs from Google Maps, stitching them together in Photoshop and scaling them made me realise a few things – I had to cut out areas which weren't vital to the location.

Looking East along the coast, the significant inroads made into the mountain by years of quarrying can be seen. For decades, Penmaenmawr supplied the national network with ballast.

The first element to keep was the stone crushing plant, a large concrete structure which in model form at 70cm in height would make an imposing structure. Its small wagon loader too would be modelled which pivots on an arc to evenly load wagons. Making this work as a feature at one end of the layout provides entertainment between trains on the mainline. At this end of the layout, an overbridge makes a useful scenic break to the fiddle yard.

At the other end of the layout is the signal box, but beyond that, there was little of interest worth modelling. With the layout length determined, it was time to select its width. The north Wales coast line is on a curve as it passes through Penmaenmawr and this would be represented, so to include the features I wanted on boards no wider than a metre, I had to build the layout on a curve too. The easiest solution was found to make one board angled. ■

The height of Penmaenmawr towering above the town in the background is sure to make an impressive backscene.

LONGDREM

Built in the loft of a bungalow, Eric Kidd's OO gauge layout is an adaptation of Longniddry, on the East Coast Main Line.

Factfile

Layout name: Longdrem
Scale/gauge: OO gauge
Size: 18ft x 12ft 6in
Era/region: BR (ScR) 1956-1962
Location: Fictitious somewhere around Edinburgh
Layout type: Continuous loop with central terminus
Owner: Eric Kidd
Photography: Tony Wright
See more: July & August 2009 **BRM**

Eric Kidd and his friend Tommy Mann were thinking of a location on which they could base their next layout. Either the East Coast Main Line in Scotland or the Waverley route would suit the locomotives and rolling stock that Eric owned. They looked at many locations, but came back to the usual modelling snag of a lack of space.

Eric wanted a continuous circuit to watch the trains go by, especially his Haymarket 'Pacifics' and ex-NBR locomotives, but he liked the idea of a branch line for end-to-end operation too.

They both considered that the track formation at Longniddry on the ECML, east of Edinburgh, would be feasible in the space available. Apart from being on the ECML, it was also the junction for the Haddington Branch, so the end-to-end run to and from the fiddle yard could be accommodated.

As luck would have it, shortly afterwards at a local exhibition, Eric came across an Ordnance Survey drawing of the track plan for Longniddry from the 1930s and used this as the basis with slight modifications, mainly

that of dispensing with a couple of the Down line sidings in an effort to avoid a cluttered feel to the junction.

With these changes to the plan, a name change was felt necessary, so Longdrem was chosen (Drem, a few miles further south on the ECML, being the junction for the North Berwick branch).

Eric believes it's always a conundrum when planning a layout as to whether it is better to model an actual location which can sometimes be too restrictive regarding the type of stock to run, or the flexibility of a fictional location, which has the atmosphere of the area modelled. Eric chose the latter because he's a firm believer that pragmatism is a great thing.

By placing the junction on the baseboard immediately before the baseboards containing the fiddle yard, when travelling on the Up main line, it allows for a journey

from the fiddle yard to the branch station and goods yard of practically two circuits of the layout, one being on the main line round to the junction and then crossing over to the branch.

The branch station could have been based on the Corstorphine station branch in Edinburgh, but it wouldn't fit. ■

Pros

▮ Option to run to 'PinkHill' terminus or 'Longdrem' from fiddle yard
▮ Station on curve frees space for locomotive shed and its approach
▮ Commencing points on curves before fiddleyards increases siding lengths
▮ Variety of attractive tunnels and small bridges

Cons

▮ Approach to 'Longdrem' from fiddleyard is largely representive of many parts of the East Coast Main Line, devoid of lineside architectural features with miles of fields

> **As luck would have it, Eric came across a 1930s Ordnance Survey drawing of the track plan for Longniddry, and used this as the basis with slight modifications"**

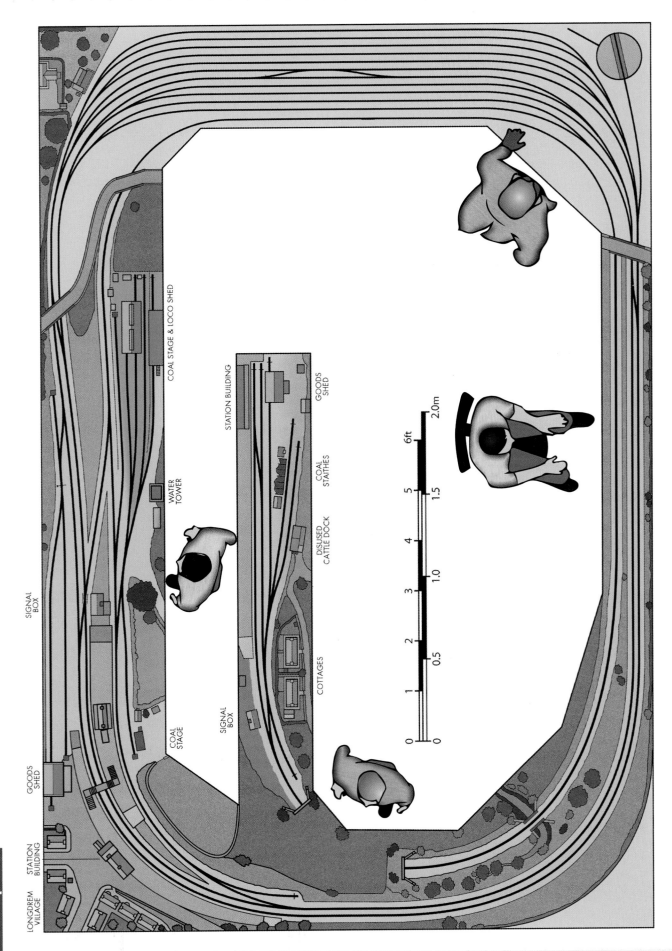

LONGDREM VILLAGE

STATION BUILDING

GOODS SHED

SIGNAL BOX

COAL STAGE

SIGNAL BOX

WATER TOWER

COAL STAGE & LOCO SHED

STATION BUILDING

GOODS SHED

COAL STAITHES

DISUSED CATTLE DOCK

COTTAGES

6ft   5   4   3   2   1   0
2.0m 1.5 1.0 0.5 0

ASTON

Martin Jeffrey's O gauge layout is designed for easy transportation and setup.

The second bedroom in Jeffrey's terraced house is a workshop, measuring just 3m x 2m, so the layout he and his friends built is kept stored in the clubroom at the Settlement Community Centre in Middlesbrough. It's here that they hold their annual exhibition.

'Aston' has to be transported and set up by four people, a big round layout was a little impractical, so instead they opted for an end-to-end layout with a 1.2m turntable at either end and a 5m section representing the countryside of Oxfordshire in the middle.

Building 'Aston' was intended primarily to be an excercise in building and engineering using different techniques and ideas and secondly as an exhibition layout. Researching the project involved drinking lots of tea and visiting many railways around the country.

The layout is a 1930s branchline layout in O gauge, which acquired its name when

Martin was looking at a map around the Oxfordshire area where he wanted the railway to be set. He noticed that as the Swindon line approached Oxford, it took a large detour to take in Witney, instead of going through a small place called Aston. Because he likes Aston Martin cars, he felt the name was right.

The design of the boards means they piggy-back each other with one set of legs

per board and lock together using 8mm bolts with finger plates welded to them and captive 'T' nuts, so no spanners are required.

At each end of the layout, the turntable boards are built using 9mm ply and each has four tracks, electrically connected using sliding brass bars that lock the boards down when in position.

The boards for 'Aston' can be transported in hatchback cars in two parts. ∎

Trackplan

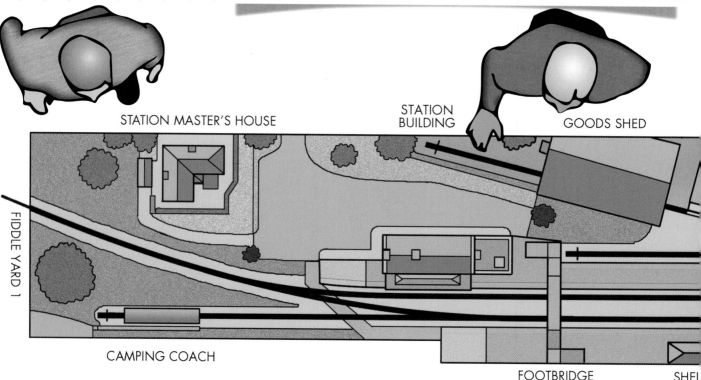

FIDDLE YARD 1

STATION MASTER'S HOUSE

STATION BUILDING

GOODS SHED

CAMPING COACH

FOOTBRIDGE

SHEL

Factfile

Layout name: Aston
Scale/gauge: O gauge
Size: 16ft x 2ft 4in
Era/region: 1930s GWR
Location: Oxfordshire
Layout type: Fiddle yard to fiddle yard
Owner: Martin Jeffrey
Photography: Ray Lightfoot
See more: September 2009 **BRM**

Pros

I Goods shed partially represented is a clever use of space
I Exiting layout on a curve adds interest, but think about fiddleyard entrance

Cons

I Platform to front of layout feels like an afterthought
I Largely symetrical trackplan design, with exception of rear sidings

" Building 'Aston' was intended to be an excercise in building and engineering using different techniques and ideas "

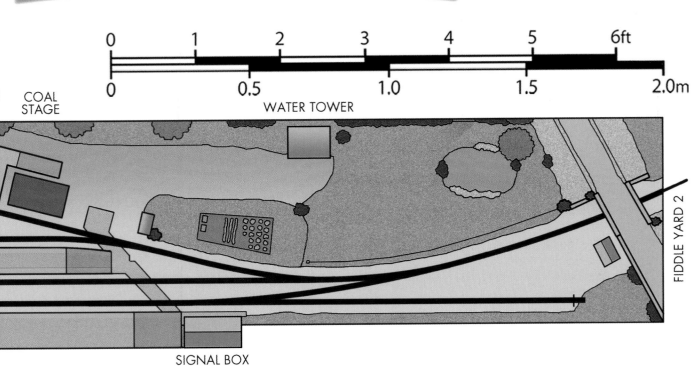

0   1   2   3   4   5   6ft

0   0.5   1.0   1.5   2.0m

COAL STAGE

WATER TOWER

FIDDLE YARD 2

SIGNAL BOX

TETLEY'S MILLS

This outstanding OO gauge creation by Dave Shakespeare depicts his boyhood memories spent in the industrial West Riding.

Factfile

Layout name: Tetley's Mills
Scale/gauge: OO gauge
Size: 23ft 6in x 9ft 6in
Era/region: BR LMR 1960s
Location: Fictitious (West Riding of Yorkshire)
Layout type: Terminus to terminus with storage
Owner: David Shakespeare
Photography: Tony Wright
See more: January 2011 **BRM**

David's first 'Tetley's Mills' layout was a continuous run. To extend the length of visible running, he incorporated a gradient to allow the track to pass over itself and had a small branch station in addition to the main through station. He used hand-built points and after the layout was completed, it was soon beginning to frustrate him as he improved his modelling standards.

Woodworm had infested a sheet of ply used as the track bed and the layout was dismantled back to the sub-base. Unfortunately he couldn't remove the gradient completely and even at a modest 1-in-60 it became problematic. It was OK if he ran at full throttle, but locomotives struggled at slow running.

Layouts on the exhibition circuit that inspired him featured atmospheric town scenes or railway architecture such as 'Runswick Bay', 'Dewsbury Midland' and 'Happisburgh'. They could hold his attention, regardless of whether or not stock was running.

For David, realism and the overall aesthetics were more important than absolute prototype accuracy. He tried to create plausible yet captivating cameos by emphasizing visually-interesting features, which hold a spectators' attention more than a prototypically accurate but dull scene.

'Tetley's Mills' is probably not really about the railway, but the scenery through which it runs. David had over 100 buildings and structures, all of which are removable. Most are on a separate base which is sunk below road or ground level. This greatly increases build time and it is not always possible to

completely disguise the joint line but is a great help for maintenance and access to hidden track.

'Tetley's Mills' depicts a busy urban terminus, built by wealthy mill owners to convey wool in and finished products out. The line is an extension to the Lancashire & Yorkshire spur from The Calder Valley line beyond Dewsbury Market Place - but links to the Great Northern route from Wakefield Westgate to Bradford, mean that the two railway companies jointly operated it. The actual line from Wakefield to Bradford was built later and at a slightly higher level and, although adjacent to the terminus, the two stations are not rail-linked. This independent, continuous circuit allows the running of lengthy coal, parcels and general mixed goods trains with the odd diverted main line Pacific-hauled express. 'Tetley's

Mills' terminus has an arrivals platform and four additional platform faces for departures, although this procedure is not strictly adhered to and all platforms can accommodate two short trains or DMUs. Access to the nearest MPD would disrupt the constant traffic on the Calder Valley line, so David incorporated a small locomotive servicing area with necessary facilities. ∎

Pros

I Lots of scenic modelling capturing the industrial grime of the West Riding area
I Removable buildings for easy access

Cons

I In David's words - 'size isn't everything' - a large layout doesn't guarantee expertise or a credible product
I Non-negligible amount of architectural modelling required

 Trackwork is commercial - Peco code 100 on the continuous circuit and storage areas for durability, code 75 at Tetley's Mills and the Barden Road branch"

Trackplan

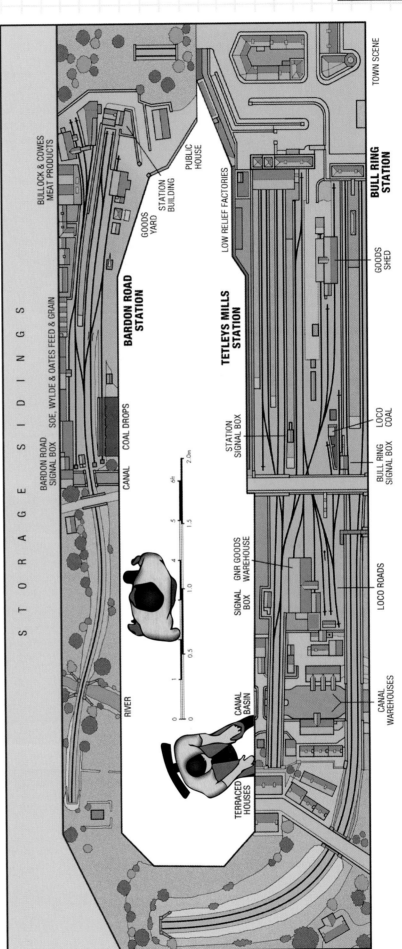

STORAGE SIDINGS

BULLOCK & COWES
MEAT PRODUCTS

SOE, WYLDE & OATES FEED & GRAIN

BARDON ROAD
SIGNAL BOX

CANAL   COAL DROPS

GOODS
YARD

STATION
BUILDING

PUBLIC
HOUSE

BARDON ROAD
STATION

LOW RELIEF FACTORIES

TETLEYS MILLS
STATION

TOWN SCENE

BULL RING
STATION

GOODS
SHED

LOCO
COAL

BULL RING
SIGNAL BOX

STATION
SIGNAL BOX

SIGNAL   GNR GOODS
BOX   WAREHOUSE

LOCO ROADS

CANAL
WAREHOUSES

RIVER

CANAL
BASIN

TERRACED
HOUSES

0   0.5   1   1.0   4   5   6H   2.0m
0   0.5   1.0   1.5

TRENTHAM JUNCTION

A new house with a large loft enabled John White to build his dream Eastern Region layout to re-kindle the memories of his youth.

Factfile

Layout name: Trentham Junction
Scale/gauge: OO gauge
Size: 27ft x 12ft
Era/region: BR Eastern Region 1958-1964
Location: Fictitious
Layout type: Continuous loop
Owner: John White
Photography: Ray Lightfoot

Trentham Junction is a fictional main line railway set in the north of England in the time capsule of 1958-1964. The layout name was inspired by its close proximity to the River Trent when the railway was first envisaged. Being born in a traditional railway family at Doncaster, with most close members of his family working at the railway workshops, affectionately known as 'The Plant', choosing the Eastern Region and its locomotives was a done deal for John.

When it came to moving house, he decided to purchase a property with a large space to accommodate his needs, resulting in a railway room in a loft offering a 37ft x 12ft space.

Designing his layout had to meet two criteria: to enable its use at home with viewing taking place from its inside and to make it transportable in the event of taking it to exhibitions where viewing from the outside would take place. With a large locomotive fleet, a Motive Power Depot for steam and diesel locomotives, a goods shed and carriage stabling was high on his list of requirements.

The space allocated for the layout is 27ft x 12ft, allowing a continuous loop design for the mainline with a minimum radii of 4ft.

After considerations, John opted not to exhibit the layout, which released him from the constraints of keeping points away from baseboard joins. A prototypical sequence is used to run trains, avoiding congestion on running lines or operational mistakes. ∎

Pros

✓

I Action-packed and filled with sidings, this layout is ideal for more than one operator
I Layout is designed to be viewed from all sides, inside and out

Cons

✗

I Three-link couplings are prone to buffer lock on curves of less than 4ft radii
I A need for further carriage sidings was identified
I No off-scene storage makes alternating motive power on rolling stock laborious

> "When it came to moving house, John decided to purchase a property with a large space, resulting in a railway room in a loft offering a 37ft x 12ft space"

OO
GAUGE

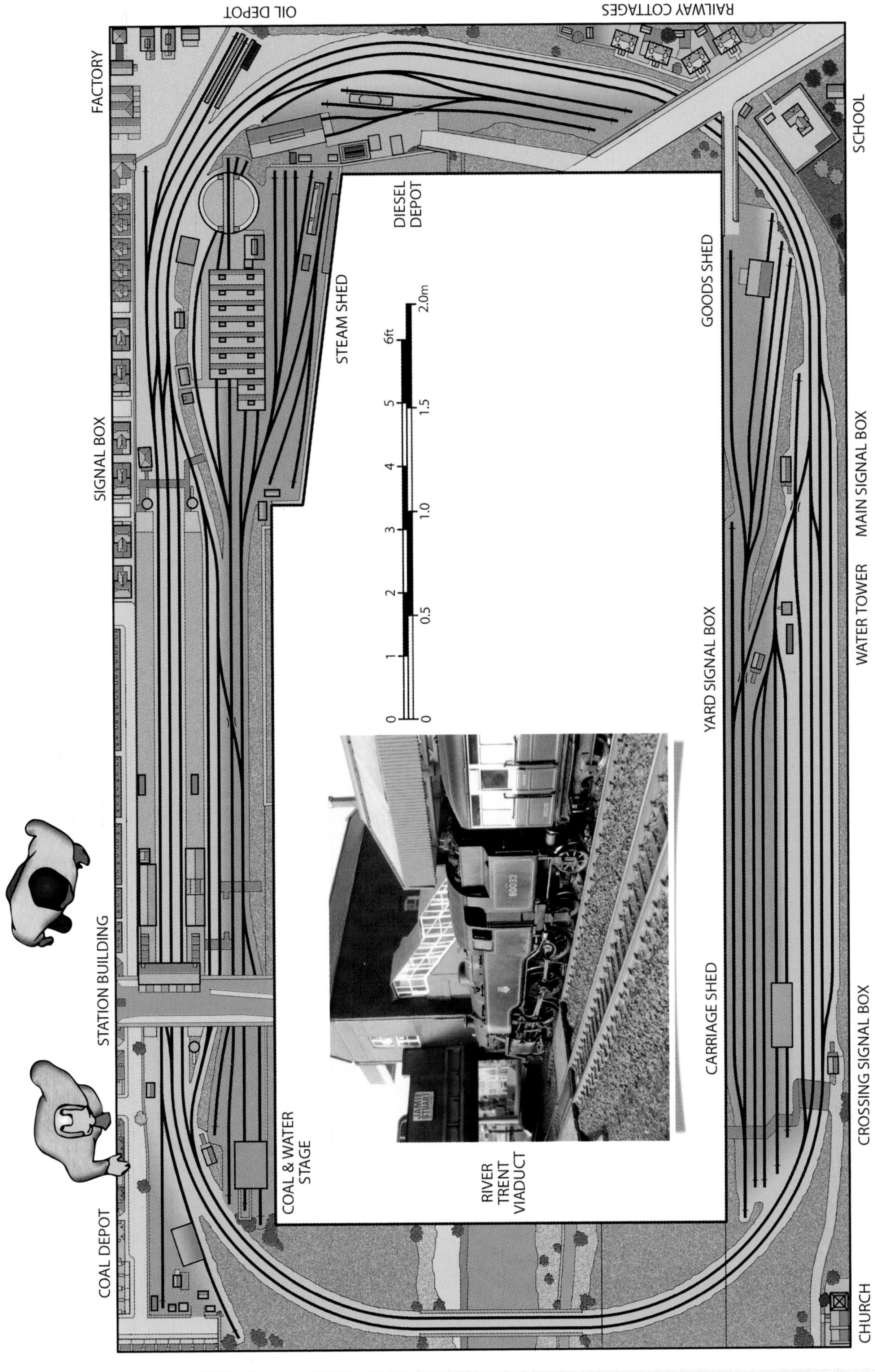

OIL DEPOT

FACTORY

RAILWAY COTTAGES

SCHOOL

SIGNAL BOX

DIESEL
DEPOT

STEAM SHED

GOODS SHED

MAIN SIGNAL BOX

WATER TOWER

YARD SIGNAL BOX

STATION BUILDING

CROSSING SIGNAL BOX

COAL DEPOT

COAL & WATER
STAGE

CARRIAGE SHED

RIVER
TRENT
VIADUCT

CHURCH

0   1   2   3   4   5   6ft

0   0.5   1.0   1.5   2.0m

ELGIN

Ted Burt chose an unusual Scottish prototype as the basis for his all-action exhibition layout.

Factfile

Layout name: Elgin
Scale/gauge: N gauge
Size: 11ft 4in x 8ft
Era/region: 1980s/1990s BR ScR
Location: Scottish Highlands
Layout type: Continuous loop
Owner: Ted Burt
Photography: Tony Wright
See more: October 2009 **BRM**

N gauge (1:148 scale) allows a good deal to be modelled in a given space. To be able to model trains running through a landscape, Ted believed that N gauge gives the widest options for most people.

Ted's wishlist for an exhibition was that it should depict the 1980-1990 era, offer a variety of rolling stock with freight and passenger operations, have potential for shunting and be constructed with a view to exhibiting it.

Scanning books and railway magazines, he found that the Inverness to Aberdeen line, in particular Elgin , fulfilled these requirements. With his location and era chosen, Ordnance Survey maps were bought and consulted and a trackplan was drawn using this information alongside various photographs and video footage. The resulting plan suggested that 10ft was necessary to model the freight yard and around 6ft for the passenger station.

The road bridge to the east of the station was chosen as the location to 'distort' the trackplan from the relatively straight Inverness-Aberdeen prototype. The track is curved to either side of the bridge on the model and so the main line runs closer to the freight yard than in reality.

The modern station building was fairly straightforward, but the GNoSR station has a square section tower which transforms into a circular section with coned slate roof turret.

Wiring on 'Elgin' is kept relatively simple and the layout is controlled by a Gaugemaster UD panel-mounted twin-track unit, powered from a Gaugemaster M1 cased transformer. The goods yard is operated

from 'track 1' and the mainline from 'track 2'. Electrical connection across board joins is by means of double terminal (male/female) screw strip connectors. The main line is singled beyond the passing loop of the station lines, so trains are isolated in the loop until the single section is cleared by the train from the other direction.

Points on the fiddleyard are Peco Insulfrog, so only the line set is powered, but each 'half' (Up or Down) can be isolated using miniature switches. ■

Pros

I Running lines extend round side of the layout at the Inverness side of the layout
I Generous storage roads allow good variety of rolling stock to be displayed

Cons

I Wire in tube points sometimes prone to damage in transit
I DCC would simplify operation and remove the need for isolation switches

 Ordnance Survey maps were bought and consulted and a trackplan was drawn using this information alongside various photographs and video footage

Trackplan

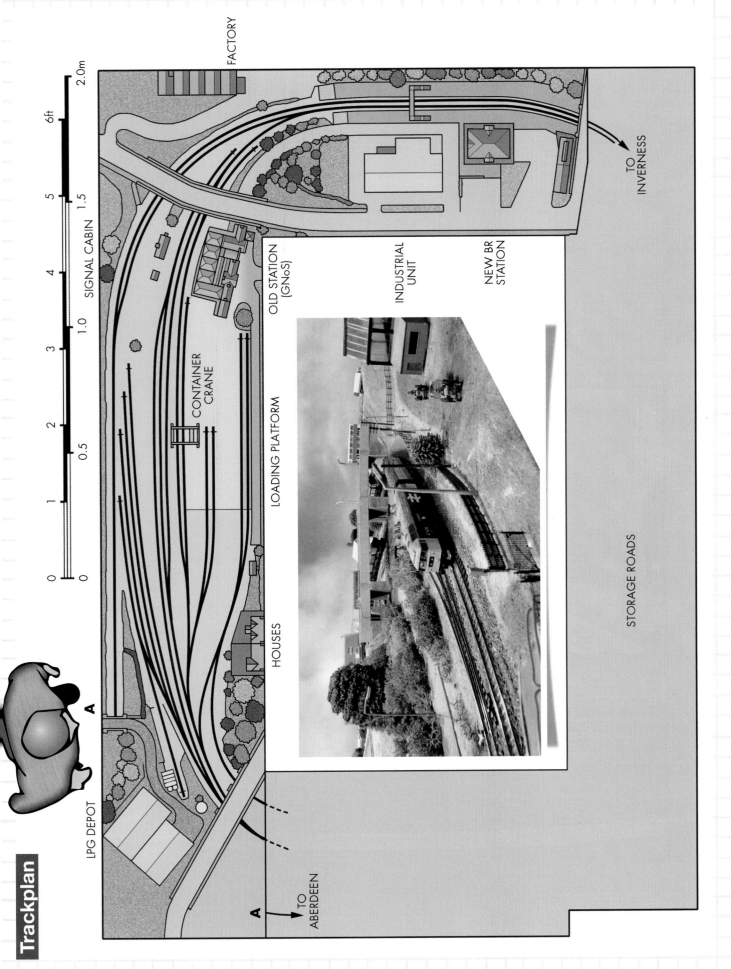

FACTORY

SIGNAL CABIN

2.0m

6ft

1.5

1.0

0.5

CONTAINER
CRANE

LOADING PLATFORM

HOUSES

LPG DEPOT

A

A

TO
ABERDEEN

OLD STATION
(GNoS)

INDUSTRIAL
UNIT

NEW BR
STATION

TO
INVERNESS

STORAGE ROADS

KINETON

Leamington & Warwick Model Railway Society members describe how research material was turned into a trackplan for their new layout.

FACTFILE

| Scale/Gauge: 2mm:1ft scale, 9.42mm gauge 2FS
| Dimensions: 12ft by 2ft, tapering to 1ft
| Era: 1948-52
| Region/Location: LMR, South Warwickshire
| Layout Type: End-to-end
| Power/Control: DCC

Photographs of Kineton in BR days are scarce, but on April 24, 1955, ex-GWR 'Dukedog' 4-4-0 No. 9015 paused there with the REC's 'South Midlander' railtour. Obscure for most of its life. the 'SMJ' became popular for railtours in its later years, even getting a visit from a Southern 'N' 2-6-0 and Bulleid Q1 on another occasion.
A.W. CROUGHTON / RAIL ARCHIVE STEPHENSON

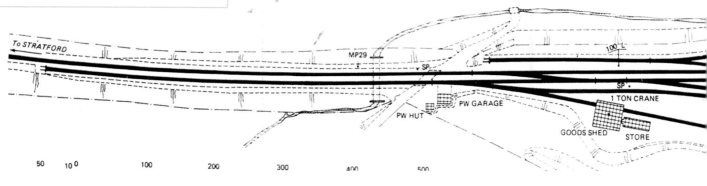

Examples of the limited selection of period photographs of Kineton the group has unearthed from various sources.

Leamington & Warwick Model Railway Society is a thriving club with approximately 70 members. During the past ten years its N gauge layout analogue layout 'Meacham' with complex wiring that required excessive maintenance was due for replacement.

SETTING OBJECTIVES

Discussions about a new layout over a period of two years lured the group to model a real location. The club's N gauge group had grown and to maintain the interest of new members it was essential to share existing experience across the group. Existing members wanted to develop their own skills by tackling new things, so the group accepted the challenge of building to 2mm finescale standards.

Designed from the start for exhibition use, the operation of the layout had to keep the watching public interested at all times. On a quiet country branch it might prove difficult, so a location was chosen with facilities to allow two trains to pass. It also required a

goods facility, providing the ability to drop off and shunt wagons.

The group considered locations on what is commonly known as the Stratford-upon-Avon & Midland Junction Railway (SMJ), although its name changed frequently during its existence. The line opened as the East & West Junction Railway (EWJR), existed as the 'SMJ' from 1909, became part of the LMS in 1923 and was taken over by BR in 1948. The group chose Kineton as the focus of the project.

Kineton lies five miles from the L&WMRS clubhouse and was opened as part of the SMJ's predecessor, the EWJR, in June 1871. A modest little station, it consisted of a good sized ticket hall, a signalbox, goods shed and five sidings that - in addition to regular goods traffic - accommodated the transportation of livestock and coal.

Kineton closed to passengers in 1952, although goods trains continued until 1963. With the exception of a short section used by the Ministry of Defence (MoD), all through services were withdrawn in 1966.

Today the location has been redeveloped as a business park, and the only remnant of the original station is the bridge carrying the Kineton to Wellesbourne road over the former railway cutting.

DETAILED RESEARCH

Although several books have been published about the 'SMJ', a limited amount of information about Kineton could be gathered from them, so more in-depth research was needed.

Warwickshire County Archives proved a useful source of information on the 'SMJ', but much of the data gathered was not specific to Kineton and it frequently raised more questions than it answered. Information about the station was limited, but the group found useful material.

Whilst local archives proved less fruitful than was hoped, one member made numerous visits to both the National Archives at Kew and the British Library and unearthed a wealth of useful information

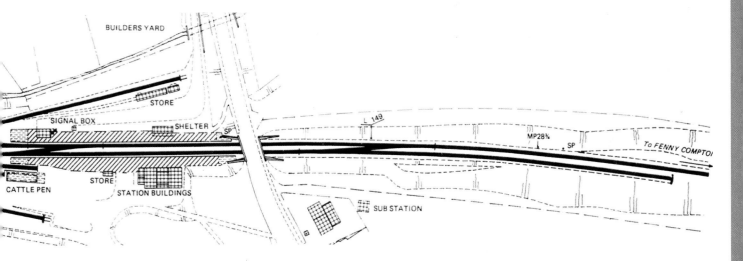

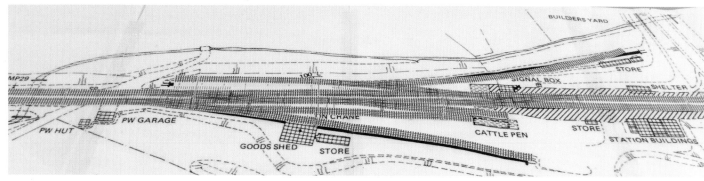

A trackplan generated in Templot was overlaid on a scale printout of an OS map to give the correct positions for the buildings and earthworks.

including timetables, schedules and SMJR staff records. Another valuable source proved to be the SMJ Society (www.smj.me) whose members gather items of interest.

OPERATING STANDARDS

The 'SMJ' offers numerous interesting locations for the railway modeller. There are many small local stations, interesting landscapes and geographical features. At various times there have been other historically interesting subjects such as the Edgehill Light Railway and ropeway and a large military ordnance depot with an internal railway system extending to over 90 miles. Some members of the group drew attention to landscape features such as the meanderings of a stream with a railway bridge over a track bridge over the stream. Although not a particularly interesting railway feature, it's an unusual landscape.

TRACKPLAN DESIGN

Research uncovered at least three variations of the trackplan throughout the life of the station (1884, 1922 and 1964). Before designing baseboards, the group adopted the 1922 version as a 'best fit' for the era they planned to model.

To turn the research into a model trackplan the group identified trackplan software products, but because they were to handbuild their track and most options only providing 'pick and place' templates, they chose to use Templot (www.templot.com).

SCALE REPLICA

To confirm the accuracy of their plans, the group built half-size replicas of the baseboards in foamboard, at which point we were able to test the track positioning by printing a half-size plan of the layout on paper.

The group looked at the site topography which has changed in recent years with the building of an industrial park. On the ground there are few landmarks remaining

other than the original roadbridge which crossed the railway at the end of the platforms. Much of the land beyond has been levelled and it isn't obvious that the railway ran around the north end of the village in a cutting on its way east towards Fenny Compton.

The club members resolved the topography as best they could using internet satellite images overlaid with a 1905 Ordnance Survey map which showed the detailed station layout at that date. The main line formed a gentle 'S' bend over the full length of the trackplan, providing the final piece in the puzzle of how to lay the track out across the baseboards. By positioning

the track at a slight diagonal over the central board, track leaving the layout at the far end of each end board could be positioned centrally and at right angles to the baseboard joins. The SMJ was a single track railway, so the use of a standard end interface made it practical to build common fiddleyard components for use at either end of the layout. A design was created to allow for multiple roads on a sliding cassette unit which would move across the baseboard to either send or receive trains despatched from the station. The inclusion of a cassette system, under development, will allow for greater variety of stock to be deployed from either end.

> ## To turn the research into a model trackplan the group identified computer software products"

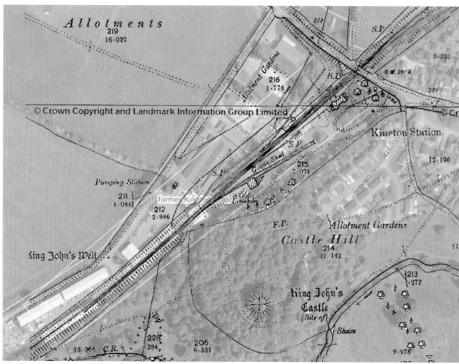

An old OS map was also superimposed on modern aerial photography of the site taken from Google Earth.

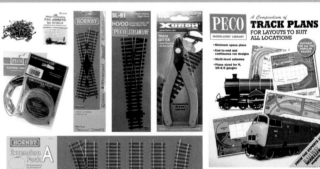

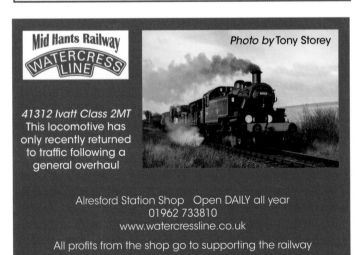

ADVERTISERS' INDEX

Jacksons Models	121
Little Layouts	115
Locomotion	8
Lord & Butler	119
Macs Model Railroading	8
Mad About Trains	116
Magnet Insurance	8
Malc's Models	121
Mid Hants Railway	118
Millenium Models	115
Model Railway Solutions	117
Modula Layouts	115
Monk Bar Model Shop Ltd	116
MVL Bridges	10
North Pitton Works	120
Peters Spares Model Railways Ltd	115
Quality Backscenes	117 & 119
Rails Of Sheffield	11
Ron Lines	116
Sawyer Models	116
Skytrex Ltd	116
South Eastern Finecast	118
The 4D Modelshop	118
The Hobby Shop	118
The Locoshed	113
The Model Shop (Exeter)	121
TMC Custom Finish Locomotives	9
Topp Trains	118
Tri-angman	121
Tutbury Models	121
Wellingborough Trains & Models	121
White Rose Modelworks	31
You Choos	114
3cp-tools	121
3mm Scale Model Railways	121
A C Models	31
Alphagraphix	115
Alton Model Centre	117
Bournemouth Model Railway	119
Branchlines	118
Buoys Toys & Models	121
C & M Models	118
Cheltenham Model Centre	113
CMASModels	31
Coastal DCC	31
Crafty Hobbies	118
Culcheth Model Railways	6
DB Models	111
DCC Concepts Pty Ltd	123
DCC Fitting Ltd	6
Derek's Transport Books	121
Durham Trains Of Stanley	121
Expo Drills & Tools	2 & 3
Frizinghall Models & Railways	114
Gaugemaster.Com	124
GDMK Images	118
GFB Designs (Sig-na Trak)	117
Ghost-Signs	119
Graeme Simmonds	10
Great Eastern Toys & Models	118
Grimy Times	119
Harburn Hobbies	113
Haslington Models	121
Hatton's Model Railways	122
Hornby Hobbies Ltd	64 & 65
Items Mail Order Ltd	121

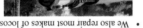
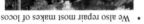

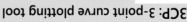

How to get started?

Hattons Est.1946 • MODEL RAILWAYS •

1. Planning

The first stage of your model railway is planning the design and layout of your trackwork.

We have a range of track planning books and software available from Hornby, Peco and many more available at:

www.hattons.co.uk/planning

2. Track

Track is arguably the most important element of your railway. We stock the full range of Hornby and Peco track in OO, N and O gauges, including pointwork.

We also stock everything else you need for your track including fixing pins and underlay to keep the noise down.

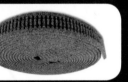

3. Electrics

From power supplies to point motors and switches to wire. We've got everything you could possibly need to get up and running in no time.

Not sure where to start? Get in touch and one of our experts will be more than happy to help you out.

4. Control

Happy running one loco at a time on your layout? Analogue will suit you fine.

Want to perform more complex, multi-loco movements? Digital (DCC) will be perfect for you.

We've got a range of controllers to suit everyones preferences and budget.

5. Scenery

Scenery is often one of the least appreciated element of making a model railway. Something as simple as adding a tunnel or a station can add extra excitement to your layout.

We've got the entire range including: ballast, figures, buildings, trees and much more.

6. Locos & Stock

Locos and rolling stock are where you can really have some fun on your layout. Do you want to run a particular period in history or anything that takes your fancy?

We get all the latest releases in from: Hornby, Bachmann, Heljan and Dapol as well as having a huge selection of pre-owned items.

Hattons Model Railways, 17 Montague Road, Widnes, WA8 8FZ
0151 733 3655   www.hattons.co.uk   info@hattons.co.uk